Grammar Links Basic

An Introductory Course for Reference and Practice

Linda Butler

D0139242

M. Kathleen Mahnke

Series Editor
St. Michael's College

Houghton Mifflin Company   Boston   New York

Publisher: Patricia A. Coryell

Director of ESL: Susan Maguire

Senior Development Editor: Kathleen Sands Boehmer

Editorial Assistant: Evangeline Bermas

Senior Project Editor: Kathryn Dinovo

Manufacturing Manager: Florence Cadran

Marketing Manager: Annamarie Rice

Marketing Associate: Laura Hemrika

Cover image: Stock Illustration Source © 2003 David Ridley, *Multicultural Figures*

Photo credits: p. 11, Cassy Cohen/PhotoEdit; p. 19(a) David Young-Wolff/ PhotoEdit; p. 19(b), Daniel Bosler/Getty Images; p. 19(c), Michael Newman/ PhotoEdit; p. 19(d), David Young-Wolff/PhotoEdit; p. 41, Lawrence Migdale/ Stock Boston; p. 48(a), David Young-Wolff/PhotoEdit; p. 48(b), David Young-Wolff/PhotoEdit; p. 48(c), Spencer Grant/Stock Boston; p. 48(d), Michael Justice/The Image Works; p. 48(e), Bill Aron/PhotoEdit; p. 48(f), David Young-Wolff/PhotoEdit; p. 49, Spencer Grant/Stock Boston; p. 56, David Young-Wolff/PhotoEdit; p. 75, George Shelley/Corbis; p. 82, Susan Van Etten/ PhotoEdit; p. 100(a), Tony Sanno/The Image Works; p. 100(b), Peter Grumann/ Getty Images; p. 111, PhotoDisc/Getty Images; p. 120(a) Myrleen Ferguson Cate/PhotoEdit; p. 120(b), Rob Levine/Corbis; p. 120(c), David Young-Wolff/ PhotoEdit;, p. 149, Digital Vision/Getty Images; p. 185, Nathan Bilow/Getty Images; p. 206, Mug Shots/Corbis; p. 219, Elena Rooraid/PhotoEdit.

Printed in the U.S.A.

Library of Congress Control Number: 2002101699

ISBN-13: 978-0-618-15026-7   ISBN-10: 0-618-15026-9

3456789-DBH-07

Contents

Welcome to Grammar Links!   x

Acknowledgments   xv

To the Student   xvi

Introduction: Useful Words and Expressions   1

Hi!   1

The Letters of the Alphabet   2

Cursive Letters   3

Names   4

Where Are You From?   5

Numbers   7

Telling Time   8

Words for the Classroom   9

UNIT 1: At School   11

Chapter 1: New Friends   12

Grammar Briefing 1: Subject Pronouns *I, You, He, She* and *It*   14

Grammar Briefing 2: Present Tense of *Be* with *I, You, He, She,* and *It*   15

Grammar Briefing 3: Possessive Adjectives *My, Your, His,* and *Her*   16

Grammar Briefing 4: *Who, What, Where*   18

Extra Practice   20

Chapter 2: The Classroom   22

Grammar Briefing 1: Nouns   24

Grammar Briefing 2: Plural Subject Pronouns + *Be;* Plural Possessive Adjectives   28

Grammar Briefing 3: *There Is* and *There Are*   30

Grammar Briefing 4: *This* and *These*   31

Extra Practice   33

Unit 1 Wrap-Up Activities   35
Grammar Summary   37
Test Yourself   39

UNIT 2: At Home   41

Chapter 3: Families   42

Grammar Briefing 1: Negative Statements with *Be*   44
Grammar Briefing 2: Questions and Answers with *Be*   46
Grammar Briefing 3: Present Tense of *Have*—Affirmative Statements   49
Grammar Briefing 4: Questions and Answers with *Do You Have*   51
Extra Practice   53

Chapter 4: Nice Eyes and a Great Smile   55

Grammar Briefing 1: The Article *A/An*   57
Grammar Briefing 2: *This, That, These, Those*   59
Grammar Briefing 3: Descriptive Adjectives   61
Grammar Briefing 4: Possessive Nouns   64
Extra Practice   67

Unit 2 Wrap-Up Activites   69
Grammar Summary   71
Test Yourself   73

UNIT 3: Busy People   75

Chapter 5: What Are You Doing?   76

Grammar Briefing 1: Present Progressive Tense—Affirmative Statements   78
Grammar Briefing 2: Spelling *-ing* Verb Forms   81
Grammar Briefing 3: Present Progressive Questions   83
Grammar Briefing 4: More About Plural Nouns   88
Extra Practice   91

Chapter 6: What About You?   93

Grammar Briefing 1: Present Progressive Tense— Negative Statements   95

Grammar Briefing 2: Affirmative and Negative Statements with *Can*   97

Grammar Briefing *3*: *Yes/No* Questions with *Can*   99

Grammar Briefing 4: *And, But*, and *Or*   100

Extra Practice   103

Unit 3 Wrap-Up Activities   105

Grammar Summary   107

Test Yourself   109

UNIT 4: Everyday Life   111

Chapter 7: Daily Routines   112

Grammar Briefing 1: Simple Present Tense—Affirmative Statements   114

Grammar Briefing 2: Simple Present Tense Verbs after Third Person Singular Subjects   116

Grammar Briefing 3: Simple Present *Yes/No* Questions and Short Answers   120

Grammar Briefing 4: Present Progressive vs. Simple Present   124

Extra Practice 127

Chapter 8: Would You Like Something?   129

Grammar Briefing 1: Simple Present Tense—Negative Statements   131

Grammar Briefing 2: Simple Present Tense—*Wh-* Questions and Answers   133

Grammar Briefing 3: Adverbs of Frequency   136

Grammar Briefing 4: *Would You Like* and *I'd Like*   138

Extra Practice   141

Unit 4 Wrap-Up Activities   143

Grammar Summary   145

Test Yourself   147

UNIT 5: Going Places   149

Chapter 9: It's Sunny and Warm   150

Grammar Briefing 1: *It* + the Time, Day, Date, or Weather   152

Grammar Briefing 2: Prepositional Phrases; Prepositions for Describing Time   155

Grammar Briefing 3: Prepositions for Describing Location or Place   158

Grammar Briefing 4: Object Pronouns   161

Extra Practice   163

Chapter 10: Eating Out   165

Grammar Briefing 1: Count and Noncount Nouns; The Indefinite Article *A/An*   167

Grammar Briefing 2: The Definite Article *The*   170

Grammar Briefing 3: Questions with *Is There/Are There*   172

Grammar Briefing 4: Quantifiers *Many, Much, A Lot of, Some, Any, A Few, A Little*; Questions with *How Many/ How Much*   174

Extra Practice   177

Unit 5 Wrap-Up Activities   179

Grammar Summary   181

Test Yourself   183

UNIT 6: Looking Back   185

Chapter 11: What a Weekend!   186

Grammar Briefing 1: The Simple Past Tense of *Be*   188

Grammar Briefing 2: Questions with *Was/Were*   191

Grammar Briefing 3: The Simple Past of Regular Verbs   194

Grammar Briefing 4: The Simple Past of Irregular Verbs   197

Extra Practice   199

Chapter 12: Long Ago   201

Grammar Briefing 1: *Yes/No* Questions in the Simple Past   203

Grammar Briefing 2: Negative Statements in the Simple Past   205

Grammar Briefing 3: More Irregular Verbs   207
Grammar Briefing 4: *Wh-* Questions in the Simple Past   209
Extra Practice   211

Unit 6 Wrap-Up Activities   213
Grammar Summary   215
Test Yourself   217

UNIT 7: Let's Look Ahead   219

Chapter 13: Looking Forward to the Future   220

Grammar Briefing 1: Expressing the Future with *Be Going To*   222
Grammar Briefing 2: Future Time Expressions   224
Grammar Briefing 3: *Yes/No* Questions with *Be Going To*   225
Grammar Briefing 4: *Wh-* Questions with *Be Going To*   227
Extra Practice   230

Chapter 14: Plans and Predictions   232

Grammar Briefing 1: Expressing the Future with *Will*   234
Grammar Briefing 2: Questions with *Will*   236
Grammar Briefing 3: *Will* vs. *Be Going To*   238
Grammar Briefing 4: *Have To*   240
Extra Practice   243

Unit 7 Wrap-Up Activities   245
Grammar Summary   247
Test Yourself   249

Appendixes   A–1
Test Yourself Answer Key   ANS–1
Tapescript   T–1
Index to the Grammar   I–1

Welcome to Grammar Links!

Grammar Links is a comprehensive five-level grammar reference and practice series for students of English as a second or foreign language. The series meets the needs of students from the beginning through the advanced level:

- *Grammar Links Basic* . . . . beginning
- *Grammar Links 1* . . . . high beginning
- *Grammar Links 2* . . . . intermediate
- *Grammar Links 3* . . . . high intermediate
- *Grammar Links 4* . . . . advanced

Grammar Links student texts are accompanied by a variety of ancillary materials, including an audiocassette or audio CD package, a teacher's manual, and a CD-ROM for extra practice. *Grammar Links 1–4* are also accompanied by a workbook. In addition, the Houghton Mifflin ESL web site provides further resources for teachers and students.

TO THE TEACHER

Series Approach

Recent research in applied linguistics tells us that when a well-designed communicative approach is coupled with a systematic treatment of grammatical form, the combination is a powerful pedagogical tool. *Grammar Links* is such a tool. *Grammar Links'* grammar explanations are clear, accurate, and carefully sequenced. All points introduced are practiced in exercises, and coverage is comprehensive and systematic. In addition, each grammar point is carefully recycled and reused in a variety of contexts.

The grammar in *Grammar Links Basic* is presented in small manageable chunks arranged with students' communicative needs in mind. Each unit in *Grammar Links Basic* also treats a general topic of easy accessibility. "Unit One: At School," for example, teaches language for the classroom along with the grammar. "Unit Four: Everyday Life" teaches the simple present in the context of the daily routines of people at home, at school, and at work.

The communicative framework of *Grammar Links 1–4* is that of the theme-based approach to language learning. Unlike other approaches, theme-based models promote the development of both cognitive and linguistic abilities through in-depth contextualization of language in a content area. In *Grammar Links 1–4*, content serves as more than a backdrop for communication; high-interest topics are presented and developed along with the grammar of each chapter. As a result, *Grammar Links 1–4* exercises and activities are content-driven as well as grammar-driven. While learning about adjective clauses in Book 3, for example, students explore various aspects of the discipline of psychology. While they are practicing gerunds and infinitives in Book 2, they read about successful American entrepreneurs. And, while practicing the simple present tense in Book 1, students learn about and discuss North American festivals and other celebrations. Throughout the series, students communicate about meaningful content, transferring their grammatical training to the English they need in their daily lives.

In short, the *Grammar Links* approach provides students with the best of all possible language learning environments—systematic treatment of grammar within a communicative theme-based framework.

About the Books

Grammar coverage in the *Grammar Links* series has been carefully designed to spiral across levels. Structures introduced in one book are recycled and built upon in the next. Students not only learn increasingly sophisticated information about the structures but also practice these structures in increasingly challenging contexts. Themes show a similar progression across levels, from less academic at the beginning levels to more academic in Book 3 and Book 4.

Grammar Links is flexible in many ways and can be easily adapted to the particular needs of users. Although its careful spiraling makes it ideal as a series, the comprehensive grammar coverage at each level means the individual books can also stand alone. The careful organization also makes it possible for students to use their text as a reference after they have completed a course. The units in a book can be used in the order given or can be rearranged to fit the teacher's curriculum. Books can be used in their entirety or in part. In addition, the inclusion of ample practice allows teachers to be selective when choosing exercises and activities. All exercises are labeled for grammatical content, so that structures can be practiced more or less extensively, depending on class and individual needs.

Grammar Links Basic — Unit and Chapter Components

- **Unit Objectives.** Each unit begins with lists of objectives so that teachers and students can preview the major grammar points covered in the unit.

- **Chapter Introduction.** Each chapter opens with Grammar in Action, a conversation which introduces the grammar of the chapter in context, so that students can get a sense for how grammar is actually used by native speakers before studying it in depth. Students can both read and listen to this conversation. This contextualized material is accompanied by a grammar consciousness-raising section, Think about Grammar. In Think about Grammar tasks, students figure out some aspect of grammar by looking at words and sentences from the Grammar in Action reading/listening selection. They induce grammatical rules themselves before having those rules given to them. Think about Grammar thus helps students become independent grammar learners by promoting critical thinking and discussion about grammar.

- **Grammar Briefings.** The grammar is presented in Grammar Briefings. Each chapter has four Grammar Briefings, so that information is given in manageable chunks.

- **Grammar Hotspots.** Grammar Hotspots are a special feature of *Grammar Links*. They occur at one or more strategic points in each chapter. Grammar Hotspots focus on aspects of grammar that students are likely to find particularly troublesome. Some hotspots contain reminders about material already presented in the Grammar Briefing charts; others go beyond the charts.

- **Talking the Talk.** Talking the Talk is another special feature of *Grammar Links*. Our choice of grammar is often determined by our audience, whether we are writing or speaking, the situations in which we find ourselves, and other sociocultural factors. Talking the Talk treats these factors. Students become aware of differences between formal and informal English and between written and spoken English.

- **Practice Exercises.** Each Grammar Briefing is followed by systematic practice of all the grammar points introduced. The general progression within each set of exercises is from more controlled to less controlled, from easier to more difficult, and often from more receptive to more productive and/or more structured to more communicative. A wide variety of innovative exercise types is included in each of the four skill areas: reading, writing, speaking, and listening 🎧. The exercise types used are appropriate to the particular grammar points being practiced. For example, more drill-like exercises are often used for practice with form. More open-ended exercises often focus on function.

   In many cases, drill-like practice of a particular grammar point is followed by communicative practice of the same point, often as pair work 👥 or group work 👥👥.

   In addition, the link between grammar and writing ✍ is addressed explicitly in *Grammar Links* exercises.

- **Extra Practice.** Students at the beginning level of grammar instruction need a great deal of reinforcing practice. To this end, each chapter in *Grammar Links Basic* includes an Extra Practice section. The Extra Practice pages make ideal homework assignments.

- **Unit Wrap-Ups.** Each unit ends with a series of activities that pull the unit grammar together and enable students to practice and apply what they have learned. *Grammar Links Basic* Wrap-up tasks include reading, writing, editing, and listening/speaking activities. Through this series of open-ended tasks, which build on and go beyond the individual chapters, students get communicative practice in all skill areas.

- **Grammar Summaries.** At the end of each unit, *Grammar Links Basic* provides Grammar Summaries of all the grammar points taught in that unit.

- **Test Yourself.** Each unit ends with a Test Yourself section, which contains one test for each chapter. These tests provide both students and teachers with much-needed feedback on student progress. Test Yourself answers are included in the back of the book so that feedback and correction are immediate.

- **Appendices.** Appendices supplement the grammar presented in the Grammar Briefings. They provide students with word lists, spelling and pronunciation rules, and other supplemental rules related to the structures taught. The appendices are a rich resource for students as they work through exercises and activities.

- **Tapescript.** The script for all exercises recorded on the audiocassette/audio CD appears at the back of the text for the teacher's convenience.

Other Components of the Grammar Links *series*

- **Audiocassette/Audio CD.** All *Grammar Links* listening exercises and all unit or chapter introductions have been recorded.

- **Workbook.** Workbooks accompany *Grammar Links 1–4*. They contain a wide variety of exercise types and provide extensive supplemental self-study practice of each grammar point presented in the student texts. TOEFL® practice questions and student self-tests are also included in the workbooks.

- **Links to the World Wide Web.** The Houghton Mifflin ESL web site provides resources for the instructor such as general teaching guidelines for each book in the series, tapescripts, downloadable tests, and the answer keys for both the student books and the workbooks. For students, the site provides student practice tests and vocabulary flashcards. The site also provides links to other sites on the World Wide Web. Visit

www.hmco.com/college/ESL for grammar information and practice, teacher resources, and links to sites with further information on topics and themes featured in the texts. Links are updated frequently, to ensure that students and teachers can access the best information available on the web.

M. Kathleen Mahnke, Series Editor
Saint Michael's College
Colchester, VT

Acknowledgments

SERIES EDITOR'S ACKNOWLEDGMENTS

This edition of *Grammar Links* would not have been possible without the thoughtful and enthusiastic feedback of teachers and students. Many thanks to you all!

I would also like to thank all of the *Grammar Links* authors, from whom I continue to learn so much every day. Many thanks, as well, to the dedicated staff at Houghton Mifflin: Joann Kozyrev, Evangeline Bermas, Mira Bahrin, and Annamarie Rice.

A very special thanks to Kathy Sands Boehmer and to Susan Maguire, for their vision, their sense of humor, their faith in all of us, their flexibility, their undying tenacity, and their willingness to take risks in order to move from the mundane to the truly inspirational!

M. Kathleen Mahnke, Series Editor

AUTHOR'S ACKNOWLEDGMENTS

I am very grateful to Kathleen Mahnke for her wonderful leadership of the *Grammar Links* team and for her dual role in the creation of this book, as series editor and as developmental editor. Her expertise, sound judgment, and good humor have been invaluable. I would also like to thank Susan Maguire for her support, and for the vision and dedication that have brought about Houghton Mifflin's collection of outstanding ESL materials. My thanks also to: Kathy Sands Boehmer, Joann Kozyrev, Evangeline Bermas, Mira Bharin, and the rest of the Houghton Mifflin team for their many contributions and to Greta Sibley, Len Neufeld, and Jack Beckwith for their work on the design. In addition, I would like to thank the following reviewers, whose comments helped to shape this text: Kathleen Kelly, Passaic Community College, NJ; Darenda Borgers and Dianne Ruggiero, Broward Community College, FL; Robert Giron, Montgomery College, MD; Christie Allred, San Diego Mesa Community College, CA; Reina Welch, Miami Dade Community College, FL; Janna Kakishita, Mt. San Antonio College, CA; Gail Reynolds, Santa Barbara City College, CA; Marilyn Santos, Valencia Community College, FL; and Aimet Coriano, University of Puerto Rico, Mayaguez.

Linda Butler

To the Student

Grammar Links is a five-level series. These books will help you learn and use English grammar.

Look at the chart below. It tells about *Grammar Links Basic*. Each part of the book will help you learn the grammar and use it in speaking, listening, reading, and writing.

FEATURE	BENEFIT
Grammar in Action conversations	Introduce you to the grammar covered in a chapter
Think about Grammar exercises	Help you become an independent grammar learner
Grammar Briefings	Show the grammar rules clearly, with helpful examples
Grammar Hotspot boxes	Focus on key grammar points and problem areas
Talking the Talk boxes	Help you understand grammar in spoken English
Practice exercises	Give you practice in using the grammar, working alone or with your classmates
Vocabulary notes	Explain the meanings of words
Extra Practice sections	Give you even more practice with the grammar from the chapter
Unit Wrap-Up sections	Get you to see, hear, and use all the grammar of the unit in activities for reading, writing, listening, and speaking
Grammar Summaries	Bring together the grammar from all eight Grammar Briefings in the unit
Test Yourself sections	Let you see how well you understand the grammar (with answers at the back of the book)

Linda Butler

INTRODUCTION

Useful Words and Expressions

Hi!

PRACTICE

1. A. Listen and read.

B. Work with a partner. Practice 1A.

2. Meet your classmates.

Example   *Student A:* Hi. I'm Li.

               Student B: I'm Mustafa.

               Student A: Nice to meet you.

               Student B: Nice to meet you, too.

The Letters of the Alphabet

CAPITAL LETTERS	A B C D E F G H I J K L M N O P Q R S T U V W X Y Z

SMALL LETTERS	a b c d e f g h i j k l m n o p q r s t u v w x y z

PRACTICE

1. Listen and repeat the letters.

2. Say the letters with your teacher.

    1. a h j k   4. i y   6. q u w

    2. b c d e g p t v z   5. o   7. r

    3. f l m n s x

3. Listen and circle.

    1. (a) b c   3. g h i   5. m n o   7. s t u v

    2. d e f   4. j k l   6. p q r   8. w x y z

4. Listen.

CONSONANTS	b c d f g h j k l m n p q r s t v w x y* z

*y has a consonant sound in *you, New York,* and *yes

VOWELS	a e i o u y*

*y has a vowel sound in *happy, day,* and *Good-bye

5. Listen and write the vowels.

    1. __o__   2. ____   3. ____   4. ____   5. ____

Cursive Letters

ABCDEFGHIJKLMNOPQRSTUVWXYZ

abcdefghijklmnopqrstuvwxyz

PRACTICE

1. Write the letters.

Aa B

2. Read about capital letters.

   a. The first letter in a name is a capital letter.

   Write: *George*   NOT: *george*

   b. The first letter in a sentence is a capital letter.

   Write: *His name is George.*   NOT: *his name is george.*

   a sentence   a period

Names

PRACTICE

1. A. Listen and read.

B. Work with a partner. Practice 1A.

2. Ask the names of four classmates. Write the names.

NAMES
1.
2.
3.
4.

Where Are You From?

PRACTICE

1. A. Listen and read.

B. Work with a partner. Practice 1A.

C. With your partner, ask and answer the question *Where are you from?*

2. A. Listen and read.

Student A: Who is she?

Student B: That's Alla. She's from Russia.

Student A: Who is he?

Student B: That's Antonio. He's from Colombia.

B. Work with a partner. Practice 2A.

C. Work with a partner. Talk about your classmates. Ask, *Who is she?* and *Who is he?*
Write names and places.

MY CLASS	
NAME	HE/SHE IS FROM
_____	_____
_____	_____
_____	_____
_____	_____
_____	_____
_____	_____
_____	_____
_____	_____
_____	_____
_____	_____
_____	_____
_____	_____
_____	_____
_____	_____
_____	_____
_____	_____

My teacher's name is _____.

She/He is from _____.

Numbers

1	2	3	4	5
one	two	three	four	five
6	7	8	9	10
six	seven	eight	nine	ten

See page A1 for more numbers.

PRACTICE

1. Listen and repeat.

2. Listen and circle.

    a. 1 2 3 ④ 5   c. 1 2 3 4 5   e. 6 7 8 9 10   g. 6 7 8 9 10

    b. 1 2 3 4 5   d. 1 2 3 4 5   f. 6 7 8 9 10   h. 6 7 8 9 10

3. Listen and write.

    a. _3_   c. ____   e. ____   g. ____   i. ____

    b. ____   d. ____   f. ____   h. ____   j. ____

4. Listen and write the telephone numbers.

Note: In phone numbers, when you see 0, say "zero" or "oh."

    a. area code (_6_ _1_ _7_) _3_ _5_ _9_ - ____ ____ _0_

    b. area code (____ ____ ____) ____ ____ ____ - ____ ____ ____

    c. area code (____ ____ ____) ____ ____ ____ - ____ ____ ____

    d. area code (____ ____ ____) ____ ____ ____ - ____ ____ ____

Telling Time

What time is it?

It's 1:00.
It's one o'clock.

It's 2:05.
It's two-oh-five.

It's 3:10.
It's three-ten.

It's 5:15.
It's five-fifteen.

It's 7:30.
It's seven-thirty.

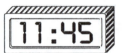

It's 11:45.
It's eleven-forty-five.

PRACTICE

1. Matching: Draw lines.

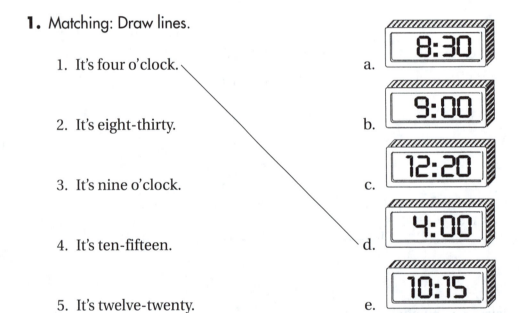

1. It's four o'clock.   a.   8:30

2. It's eight-thirty.   b.   9:00

3. It's nine o'clock.   c.   12:20

4. It's ten-fifteen.   d.   4:00

5. It's twelve-twenty.   e.   10:15

2. A. Listen and write the time.

1. __5:00__   2. _____   3. _____   4. _____   5. _____   6. _____

B. Work with a partner. Practice saying the times in 2A.

Words for the Classroom

1. **Read.**   2. **Write** your telephone number.   3. **Say** a number.

4. **Repeat** the vowels.   5. **Look at** the blackboard.   6. **Point to** a number.

7. **Ask** a question.   8. **Answer** a question.   9. **Take turns.**

PRACTICE

1. Listen and repeat the statements.

2. Listen to your teacher. Say the number of the picture.

Example   *Teacher:*   Look at the blackboard.
         Students: Number 5

3. Practice 2 with a partner. Take turns.

At School

Chapter 1
New Friends

- Subject pronouns *I*, *you*, *he*, *she*, and *it*
- The verb *be*: *am*, *is*, *are*
- Full forms and short forms (for example, *it is* ➔ *it's*, *who is* ➔ *who's*)
- Possessive adjectives *my*, *your*, *his*, and *her*
- *Wh-* question words *who*, *what*, and *where*

Chapter 2
The Classroom

- Singular and plural nouns (for example, *a student*, *two students*)
- Irregular plurals *men*, *women*, *children*, and *people*
- Common and proper nouns (for example, *city* and *Tokyo*)
- Numbers 11–30
- Subject pronouns *we*, *you*, *they* + *are*
- Possessive adjectives *our*, *your*, and *their*
- *There is* and *there are*
- *This* and *these*

CHAPTER 1

New Friends

GRAMMAR IN ACTION

Reading and Listening

A. Here are three conversations. Listen and read.

> **CONVERSATION 1**

HI. I'M DAE WON. I'M FROM KOREA.

MY NAME IS AHMET. I'M FROM TURKEY.

IT'S NICE TO MEET YOU.

IT'S NICE TO MEET YOU, TOO.

> **CONVERSATION 2**

Student 1: Who is that?

Student 2: **Her** name is Dae Won.

Student 1: Where is **she** from?

Student 2: **She's** from Seoul. It's in Korea.

> **CONVERSATION 3**

Student 1: Who is that?

Student 2: **His** name is Ahmet.

Student 1: Where is **he** from?

Student 2: **He's** from Ankara. It's in Turkey.

B. Work with a partner. Practice the three conversations in Part A. Take turns.

C. Complete.

1. What's your name? <u>My</u> _____ _____ _____ .

2. Where are you from? <u>I'm</u> _____ _____ .
your city

<u>It's</u>   <u>in</u> _____ .
your country

Think about Grammar

A. Work with a partner. Point to a picture. Ask and answer: (1) *Who's that?* and (2) *Where's he from?* or *Where's she from?* Take turns.

Example   *Student A:* Who's that?
Student B: His name is Kai.
Student A: Where's he from?
Student B: He's from China.

his/Kai	her/Parinda	his/Manuel	his/Bashar	her/Irina
he/China	she/Thailand	he/Mexico	he/Syria	she/Russia

B. Read and circle. Work alone or with a partner.

1. He is from Japan.   (**His**/Her) name is Michi.

2. She is from Bosnia.   (His/Her) name is Basarta.

3. I am from Mexico.   (My/Her) name is Maria.

4. He is from Algeria.   (His/Her) name is Paul.

5. My name is Hector.   (I'm/He's) from Panama.

6. Her name is Lucy.   (He's/She's) from Haiti.

7. His name is Yuri.   (He's/She's) from Russia.

8. Who's (he/she)?   His name is Yoshi.

C. Work in a group. Say your classmates' names and countries. Take turns.

⭐ GRAMMAR BRIEFING 1

Subject Pronouns *I, You, He, She,* and *It*

SUBJECT PRONOUNS	
I	
you	
he	
she	
it	

I am from Costa Rica.

Where are **you** from?

He is a student.   **She** is a student.   **It** is a car.

1. Subject Pronouns

Write *I, you, he, she,* or *it.* Remember capital letters.

1. His name is Yoshi. ___He___ is from Japan.

2. *Yoshi:* _____ am from Japan.

3. *Yoshi:* Where are _____ from?
   Teresa: I'm from Brazil.

4. Brazil is a country. _____ is in South America.

5. Her name is Teresa. _____ is from Brazil.

6. *Teresa:* I am from Sao Paolo. _____ is a big city.

7. His name is Bashar. _____ is a new student.

8. Her name is Nadia. _____ is from Romania.

9. *Nadia:* _____ am a new student.
   _a
   Bashar: It's nice to meet _____ .
   _b

2. Subject Pronouns

Complete.

 ## GRAMMAR BRIEFING 2

Present Tense of *Be* with *I, You, He, She,* and *It*

FULL FORM		SHORT FORM	
SUBJECT PRONOUN	*BE*	SUBJECT PRONOUN + *BE*	
I	am	I'm	**I am** a student. **I'm** a student.
you	are	you're	**You are** in my class. **You're** in my class.
he		he's	**He is** a student. **He's** a student.
she	is	she's	**She is** a student. **She's** a student.
it		it's	**It is** a Korean name. **It's** a Korean name.

 ## Grammar Hotspot!

Use *he/she/it* or a **noun** + *is*. Examples of nouns are: *Yoshi, book, student,* and *teacher.*

> **He is** a student. **Yoshi is** a student.
>
> **She is** from Boston. The **teacher is** from Boston.

3. The Present Tense of *Be*

Write *am, are,* or *is.*

1. He __is__ in my class.
2. She _____ a student.
3. I _____ a student.

4. You _____ in my class.
5. He _____ from Peru.
6. It _____ in South America.

7. Maria _____ from Cuba.
8. I _____ in class.
9. It _____ a big class.

4. Short Forms

A. <u>Underline</u> the full form. Write the short form.

He's
1. <u>He is</u> from Jordan.

2. I am at school.

3. It is nice to meet you.

4. She is here.

5. You are new here.

6. I am in the classroom.

7. It is a small room.

8. He is in my class.

9. You are in her class.

10. She is your teacher.

B. Write *I'm, you're, he's, she's,* or *it's.* Remember capital letters.

1. His name is Jack.

   <u>He's</u>_____ from Canada.

2. My name is Yoko.

   _____ from Japan.

3. Her name is Helen.

   _____ from the U.S.

4. You are new.

   _____ in this class.

5. This is my class.

   _____ in this class.

6. The classroom is small.

   _____ a small room.

7. _____ in my class.

   Nice to meet you!

8. She is a student.

   _____ from Haiti.

9. He is a student.

   _____ from Poland.

10. His name is Manuel.

    _____ a Spanish name.

⭐ GRAMMAR BRIEFING 3

Possessive Adjectives *My, Your, His,* and *Her*

SUBJECT PRONOUNS	POSSESSIVE ADJECTIVES	
I	**my**	I have a name. **My** name is Boris.
you	**your**	You have a name. What's **your** name?
he	**his**	He has a name. **His** name is Yoshi.
she	**her**	She has a name. **Her** name is Luz.

5. Possessive Adjectives *My, Your, His,* and *Her*

Write *my, your, his,* or *her.*

1. I'm a student. __My_____ name is Edgar.

2. She has a Chinese name. _____ name is Mei-Li.

3. Are you a new student? What's _____ name?

4. He has a Spanish name. _____ name is Julio.

5. Are you from Japan? Is _____ name Japanese?

6. I have a French name. _____ name is Sylvie.

7. He's Dr. Kim. _____ first name is Henry.

8. She's Dr. Tur. _____ first name is Wanda.

6. Using the Possessive Adjectives *My, Your, His,* and *Her*

Student A: Touch something near you. Ask *What's this?* Student B: Answer with words from the boxes. Take turns.

Example   *Student A:* What's this?
          Student B: It's your pen.

It's	my your his her	notebook. desk. chair. book. pen. paper. watch. backpack. _____

GRAMMAR BRIEFING 4

Who, What, Where

A. QUESTIONS WITH *BE*

WH- QUESTION WORDS	QUESTIONS		ANSWERS
who	**Who** is he?		Mr. Johnson.
			He's Mr. Johnson.
what	**What** is this?		A gift.
			It's a gift.
where	**Where** is Rome?		In Italy.
			It's in Italy.

B. SHORT FORMS WITH *BE*

FULL FORM	SHORT FORM		
Who is	**Who's**	**Who's** your teacher?	Ms. Woods.
What is	**What's**	**What's** your phone number?	525-3111.
Where is	**Where's**	**Where's** Yoshi?	In the classroom.

7. Questions and Answers with *Who, What,* and *Where*

Match.

1. What's your name?
2. Where are you from?
3. Who's he?
4. What's this?
5. Where's he from?
6. Where's the Sudan?
7. Who's she?

a. He's from the Sudan.
b. It's a map.
c. My name is Yasmin.
d. It's in Africa.
e. I'm from Taiwan.
f. That's Nadia. She's a new student.
g. That's Miguel. He's a new student.

8. Asking and Answering Questions with *Who, What,* and *Where*

Matching: Ask and answer questions with a partner. Take turns.

Student A

Who	1. . . . is your name?
What	2. . . . are you from?
	3. . . . is he?
Where	4. . . . is Tokyo?

Student B

a. His name is Miguel.
b. It's in Japan.
c. I'm from . . .
d. My name is . . .

Student B

Who	5. . . . are you from?
What	6. . . . is your name?
	7. . . . is she?
Where	8. . . . is your book?

Student A

e. I'm from . . .
f. My name is . . .
g. It's on my desk.
h. Her name is Yoko.

9. Asking and Answering Questions with *Who, What,* and *Where*

Ask and answer questions with *Who's, What's,* and *Where's.* Take turns.

Example   *Student A:* Who's this?
          Student B: Her name is Makiko.

1. Makiko
   Japan

2. a computer

3. Ms. Garcia
   the United States

4. an envelope

5. a pencil sharpener

6. Alper
   Turkey

7. Dae Won
   Korea

8. an eraser

EXTRA PRACTICE

10. Subject Pronouns + *Be*

A. Write *I, you, he, she,* or *it* + *am, is,* or *are.* Remember capital letters.

1. __He is_____ from China.

2. _____ Japanese.

3. _____ from Costa Rica.

4. _____ a new student.

5. _____ Mexican.

6. _____ in my class.

B. Write the sentences from Part A. Write short forms.

1. __He's from China._____   4. _____

2. _____   5. _____

3. _____   6. _____

11. Answering Questions with *Be*

Answer the questions. Write sentences.

1. What is her name? __Her name is Irina._____

2. Where is she from? _____

 Irina/Russia

3. What is his name? _____

4. Where is he from? _____

 Bashar/Syria

5. What is your name? _____

6. Where are you from? _____

12. Possessive Adjectives *My, Your, His,* and *Her*

Write the correct possessive adjective: *my, your, his,* or *her.*

1. I am from the Dominican Republic. <u>My</u> home is in Santiago.

2. He has a Chinese name. _____ name is Tai-Hung.

3. She is from Afghanistan. _____ name is Zeba.

4. Are you in this class? Is this _____ classroom?

5. I have a Spanish name. _____ last name is Alvarez.

6. Are you from Korea? Is _____ friend from Korea, too?

7. That's Mr. Johnson. _____ first name is George.

8. That's Ms. Jones. _____ first name is Hillary.

13. *Wh-* Questions and Answers with *Be*

Write the question and the answer for each picture.

QUESTIONS

Who is he?

Who is she?

What is this?

Where is your book?

ANSWERS

It's in my backpack.

It's a gift.

He's a new student.

Her name is Parinda.

1. Q: <u>Who is she?</u>

   A: _____

2. Q: _____

   A: _____

3. Q: _____

   A: _____

4. Q: _____

   A: _____

CHAPTER 2 — The Classroom

GRAMMAR IN ACTION

Reading and Listening

Listen and read.

Sonia:

There is	a clock a map a blackboard a computer	in our classroom.

Jenny:

There are	desks chairs books students	in our classroom.

Think about Grammar

A. Circle *There is* or *There are*.

1. (There is/There are) a blackboard in our classroom.

2. (There is/There are) desks in our classroom.

3. (There is/There are) a map in our classroom.

4. (There is/There are) notebooks in our classroom.

5. (There is/There are) students in our classroom.

6. (There is/There are) a teacher in our classroom.

B. Complete.

C. Match the sentences and the pictures.

1. This is a clock.

2. These are clocks.

3. This is a window.

4. These are windows.

5. This is a chair.

6. These are chairs.

a.

b.

c.

d.

e.

f.

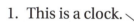

D. What's in YOUR classroom? Work with a group. Make a list.

1. _students_
2. _books_
3. _____
4. _____

5. _____
6. _____
7. _____
8. _____

9. _____
10. _____
11. _____
12. _____

23

GRAMMAR BRIEFING 1

Nouns

A. NOUNS WITH REGULAR PLURALS

SINGULAR NOUNS (SINGULAR = 1)	PLURAL NOUNS (PLURAL = 2, 3, 4, . . .)	
book	books	I have one **book**. There are two **books** on your desk.
student	students	I am a **student**. There are ten **students** in my class.

B. NOUNS WITH IRREGULAR PLURALS

SINGULAR	PLURAL	SINGULAR	PLURAL

a **man**

two **men**

a **woman**

three **women**

a **child**

four **children**

person

two **people**

C. COMMON AND PROPER NOUNS

	COMMON NOUNS	PROPER NOUNS
Words for people:	man, student, actor	**Dr. Johnson, Luz, Jackie Chan**
Words for places:	city, country, school	**Paris, Japan, Sutton High School**
Words for things:	car, soda, ocean	**Toyota, Coca-Cola, the Pacific Ocean**

1. Singular and Plural Nouns

A. Write the singular noun.

1. notebooks   a _notebook_   6. envelopes   an _____

2. children   a _____   7. blackboards   a _____

3. classrooms   a _____   8. people   a _____

4. men   a _____   9. maps   a _____

5. erasers   an _____   10. women   a _____

B. Write the plural noun.

1. a wastebasket   _wastebaskets_   4. a letter   _____

2. a calendar   _____   5. a picture   _____

3. a wallet   _____   6. a calculator _____

2. Listen for Singular and Plural Nouns

Listen to the sentences. Is the noun plural? Then add -s.

1. window   5. notebook   9. calculator

2. pictures   6. computer   10. wallet

3. letter   7. classmate   11. wastebasket

4. blackboard   8. calendar   12. pencil

3. Common and Proper Nouns

Circle the seven common nouns. (The first one is circled for you.) Underline the nine proper nouns. (The first one is underlined for you.)

This is a (picture) of my friends <u>Iva</u> and Ania. Iva is from Bosnia, and Ania is from

Poland. These women are students. They are in classes at Roxbury Community

College. The school is in the city. It's in Boston, Massachusetts.

Grammar Hotspot!

1. Use a singular noun + a singular verb. Use a plural noun + a plural verb.	The new **student is** from Japan. The new **students are** from Japan.
2. Use a noun or a pronoun, not both.	**Cristina is** from Panama. OR **She is** from Panama. NOT: Cristina ~~she~~ is from Panama.

4. Subjects + Verbs

Student A: Begin a sentence. Student B: Listen and complete the sentence. Take turns.

Example   *Student A:* Our teacher . . .
              Student B: . . . is in the classroom.

Our teacher		at school.
Our classmates		on the wall.
The students		on the desk.
The teachers	is	in the office.
The clock	are	in the classroom.
My book		in my backpack.
My pens and pencils		from the United States.

5. Numbers

Listen and repeat.

11	12	13	14	15	16	17	18	19	20
eleven	twelve	thirteen	fourteen	fifteen	sixteen	seventeen	eighteen	nineteen	twenty

21	22	23	24	25
twenty-one	twenty-two	twenty-three	twenty-four	twenty-five

26	27	28	29	30
twenty-six	twenty-seven	twenty-eight	twenty-nine	thirty

Talking the Talk

Listen to the pronunciation of these numbers:

13   /thir-TEEN/   30   /THIR-dee/

14—40   15—50   16—60   17—70   18—80   19—90

See Appendix 1 for more on numbers.

6. Listening for Numbers and Nouns

A. Listen and circle the number in the sentence.

1. (13) – 30	3. 14 – 40	5. 16 – 60	7. 18 – 80
2. 13 – 30	4. 15 – 50	6. 17 – 70	8. 19 – 90

B. Listen and write the number (from 1 to 30). Circle the noun.

1. _12_ student (students)   8. ____TV   TVs

2. ____notebook   notebooks   9. ____CD   CDs

3. ____map   maps   10. ____backpack   backpacks

4. ____piece of chalk   pieces of chalk   11. ____pen   pens

5. ____eraser   erasers   12. ____classmate   classmates

6. ____man   men   13. ____desk   desks

7. ____woman   women   14. ____name   names

7. See and Say the Number

Student A: Write a number from 1–30.
Student B: Say the number.
Take turns.

GRAMMAR BRIEFING 2

Plural Subject Pronouns + *Be*; Plural Possessive Adjectives

A. SUBJECT PRONOUNS + *BE*

SINGULAR	PLURAL
I am	**we are**
	we're
you are	**you are**
	you're
he is	**they are**
she is	**they're**
it is	

We **are** from India.
We're from India.
You are my classmates.
You're my classmates.

They **are** from Japan.
They're from Japan.

B. PLURAL POSSESSIVE ADJECTIVES

SUBJECT PRONOUNS	POSSESSIVE ADJECTIVES
we	**our**
you	**your**
they	**their**

We have a class. **Our** class is in room 126.

Lucy and Miki, are these **your** chairs?

They are new students. Ms. Tan is **their** teacher.

 ## Grammar Hotspot!

Do not add *-s* to adjectives.

These are **our books**.
NOT: These are ours books.

8. Plural Subject Pronouns

Change the <u>underlined</u> subject to *We, You,* or *They.*

We
1. <u>John and I</u> are in Nancy's class.

2. <u>These boys</u> are from China.

3. <u>You and your sister</u> are both good students.

4. <u>Jaewon and I</u> are classmates.

5. <u>The pens and papers</u> are on the desk.

6. <u>You and the teacher</u> have Spanish names.

9. Subject Pronouns *We, You,* and *They* + *Be:* Short Forms

Write *we/you/they* + *are*. Use short forms.

1. George and I are from Greece. __*We're*_____ Greek.

2. The cars are from Japan. _____ Japanese cars.

3. You and Paola are good students. _____ smart!

4. Jaewon and I are from Korea. _____ Korean.

5. These books are from the United States. _____ American.

6. You and Eva have Mr. Tye as your teacher. _____ in his class.

7. They are from Mexico. _____ Mexican.

8. My classmates and I are studying English. _____ students.

10. Using *We Are/We're* and *Our*

Work with a partner. Write true sentences about you and your partner. Use *We are/We're* and *our*. Write both your names on your papers.

11. Errors with Possessive Adjectives *Your* and *Their*

Find the eight errors and correct them. The first one is corrected for you.

1. Vi and Miki, these are ~~you're~~ *your* new books.

2. Nadia, I have papers for you and Katya. Here are yours papers.

3. Thier last name is Lan. They are sister and brother.

4. They are new students. Where are theirs classes?

5. Maria and Edgar, here are you books.

6. We have two new students. What are theirs names?

7. Where are your books? Are these you're books?

8. My friends are in Room 125. They teacher is Mrs. Cohen.

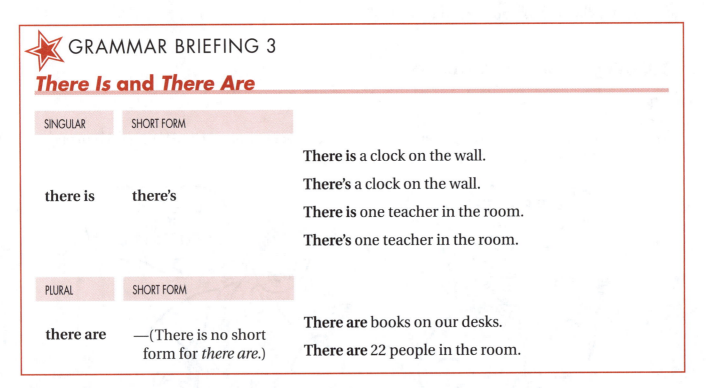

⭐ GRAMMAR BRIEFING 3

There Is and *There Are*

SINGULAR	SHORT FORM	
there is	there's	**There is** a clock on the wall. **There's** a clock on the wall. **There is** one teacher in the room. **There's** one teacher in the room.

PLURAL	SHORT FORM	
there are	—(There is no short form for *there are*.)	**There are** books on our desks. **There are** 22 people in the room.

12. There Is/There Are

Write *There is* or *There are*.

1. <u>There are</u> 18 people in the room.

2. _____ one window.

3. _____ a notebook on my desk.

4. _____ two books in my backpack.

5. _____ papers on your desk.

6. _____ an eraser on this pencil.

7. _____ pictures in this book.

8. _____ a telephone on the wall.

13. Sentences with *There Is* and *There Are*

Check (✓) the things in your classroom. Write sentences with *There's* or *There are . . . in my classroom.*

[ ] teacher   [ ] desk   [ ] student   [ ] man   [ ] woman

[ ] window   [ ] computer   [ ] clock   [ ] map   [ ] wastebasket

Examples   1. There's one teacher in my classroom.

2. There are 24 desks in my classroom

★ GRAMMAR BRIEFING 4

This and These

SINGULAR			PLURAL		
this	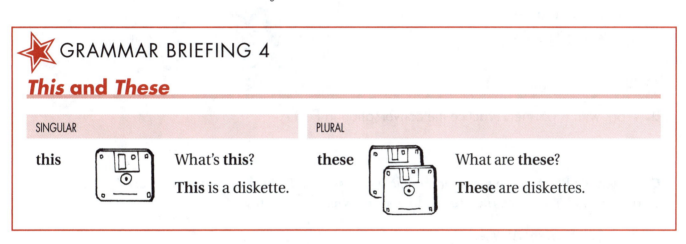	What's **this**? **This** is a diskette.	**these**		What are **these**? **These** are diskettes.

---

14. *This Is/These Are*

Write *This is* or *These are*.

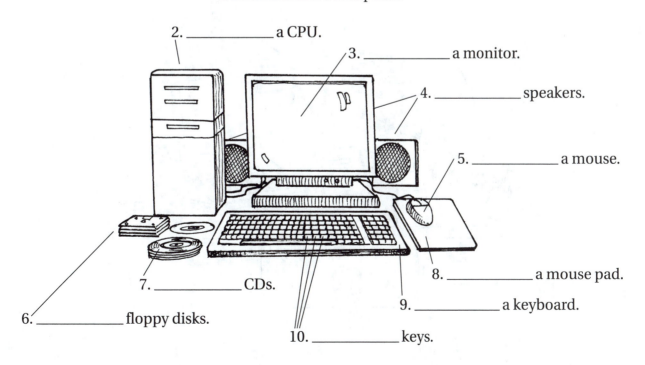

1. __This is__ a computer.

2. _____ a CPU.

3. _____ a monitor.

4. _____ speakers.

5. _____ a mouse.

6. _____ floppy disks.

7. _____ CDs.

8. _____ a mouse pad.

9. _____ a keyboard.

10. _____ keys.

15. Asking and Answering Questions with *What*

A. Listen and read.

> *Student 1:* What's this?
> *Student 2:* It's a dictionary.
> *Student 1:* What are these?
> *Student 2:* They're keys.
> *Student 1:* How do you spell that?
> *Student 2:* k-e-y-s
> *Student 1:* Thanks.

B. Work with a partner. Practice the conversation in Part A.

C. Student A: Point to something in the picture. Ask *What's this?* or *What are these?*
Student B: Use *It's . . .* or *They're . . .* in your answer. Take turns.

> Example *Student A:* What's this?
>   *Student B:* It's a CD. What are these?
>   *Student A:* They're papers.

Ask *How do you spell that?* when you need to.

EXTRA PRACTICE

16. Singular and Plural Nouns

A. Write the singular form.

1. pens   _pen_____
2. desks   _____
3. wallets   _____
4. backpacks _____
5. men   _____

B. Write the plural form.

1. pencil   _pencils_____
2. child   _____
3. woman   _____
4. computer _____
5. person   _____

17. Singular vs. Plural

Circle the correct word.

1. The books (is/are) on the teacher's desk.
2. The new (student/students) are in Room 12.
3. My pen (is/are) in my backpack.
4. The men (is/are) from Egypt.
5. The (girl/girls) is from Kuwait.
6. There are ten (woman/women) in the class.
7. My notebook (is/are) on my desk.
8. What are (this/these)?
9. This is a (gift/gifts) for you.
10. The people (is/are) at their desks.

18. Plural Subject Pronouns + *Be*

Write *we/you/they* + *are*. Remember capital letters.

1.

_____ from Japan.

2.

"_____ my classmates."

3.

"_____ from India."

19. Plural Subject Pronouns + *Be*

Write *we/you/they* + *are*. Use short forms.

1. Pedro and I are from Brazil. __We're__ Brazilian.

2. Vera and Vitek are from the Czech Republic. _____ Czech.

3. You and Tari are from Indonesia. _____ Indonesian.

4. The computers are from the United States. _____ American.

5. My classmates and I are in class. _____ in Room 125.

6. You are my classmates. _____ in my class.

7. We study at Bradford College. _____ students.

8. They teach Spanish. _____ teachers.

20. Possessive Adjectives *Our, Your, Their*

Write *our, your,* or *their*.

1. Maria and Lucy, are these __your__ books?

2. We have a teacher. _____ teacher is Ms. Rogers.

3. They have a teacher. _____ teacher is Mr. Goodman.

4. Are you new students? What are _____ names?

5. We have a classroom. _____ classroom is 248.

6. Jack and Dan have backpacks. _____ backpacks are black.

7. You and Yoko have new teachers. Who are _____ teachers?

8. The students have notebooks. _____ notebooks are blue.

21. *There Is/There Are*

Look at the picture on page 32. On a piece of paper, write sentences about the picture. Use *There is* and *There are.*

Examples   There is a desk in the picture.

There are notebooks on the desk.

Unit 1 Wrap-Up Activities

1. Juan Carlos: READING

Read this student's paragraph.

> My name is Juan Carlos. I'm from Guatemala. I'm a student at Springfield Community College. There are 24 students in my class. Our teacher is Ms. Daly. She's from New York.

2. Your Class: WRITING

Write about you and your class. Remember capital letters:
- at the beginning of a name: Ms. Daly NOT: ms. daly
- at the beginning of a sentence: There are 24 students. NOT: there are 24 students.

3. Jaewon's Class: EDITING

Correct the 10 errors. The first error is corrected for you.

> Jaewon she is from Seoul. These is a city. It is in korea. She a student at Bradley College. there is 18 student in her class. Her classmates they are from many places. There teacher is Mr. Lopez. He from California.

4. Talk about Places: SPEAKING/LISTENING

Form a group of three or four. Look at the maps on pages A9 and A10. Point to places on the map and talk about them. Take turns.

Example *Student A:* This is Florida. We are here, in Miami.

Student B: This is Colombia. My city is Bogotà. It's here.

5. A Conversation: SPEAKING/WRITING

A. Work with a partner. Look at the picture. Write a conversation.

B. Work with your partner. Act out your conversation for the class.

GRAMMAR SUMMARY

Subject Pronouns and the Verb *Be*

SINGULAR	PLURAL
I am in class. **I'm** in class.	**We are** partners. **We're** partners.
You are right. **You're** right.	**You are** partners. **You're** partners.
He is a new student. **He's** a new student.	
She is the teacher. **She's** the teacher	**They are** from Poland. **They're** from Poland.
It is a map of Japan. **It's** a map of Japan.	

★ See the Grammar Briefings on pages 14, 15, and 28.

Wh- Questions with *Be*

QUESTIONS	ANSWERS
Who is he?	His name is Miguel.
Where are you from?	I'm from Russia.
What is this?	It's a computer disk.

★ See the Grammar Briefings on pages 18 and 31.

Possessive Adjectives

SINGULAR	PLURAL
I have a book. It's **my** book.	We are in class. This is **our** classroom.
What's **your** name?	These are **your** books.
His name is Michael.	
Her name is Laura.	They have a house. It's **their** house.
I have a book. **Its** name is *Grammar Links Basic*.	

★ See the Grammar Briefings on pages 16 and 28.

Nouns

REGULAR		IRREGULAR	
SINGULAR	PLURAL	SINGULAR	PLURAL
letter	letters	person	people
boy	boys	child	children

★ See the Grammar Briefing on page 24.

There Is and There Are

SINGULAR	PLURAL
There is a map on the wall.	**There are** two maps on the wall.

★ See the Grammar Briefing on page 30.

This and These

SINGULAR	PLURAL
What's **this**? It's a pencil sharpener.	What are **these**? **These** are my notebooks.

★ See the Grammar Briefing on page 31.

TEST YOURSELF ON CHAPTER 1

1. Write the subject pronoun *I, you, he, she,* or *it*. Remember capital letters.

1. His name is Yoshi. __He__ is Japanese.
2. This is our classroom. _____ is Room 201.
3. My name is Carlos. _____ am from Panama.
4. What's your name? Where are _____ from?
5. Who is _____ ? What's his name?
6. Who is _____ ? What's her name?

2. Write *I, you, he, she, it* + the form of *be* (*am, is, are*). Use short forms.

1. That's Mr. Harris. __He's__ a teacher.
2. That's Ms. Daly. _____ a teacher.
3. My name is Xuan. _____ from Taiwan.
4. You are my classmate. _____ in my class.
5. This is my watch. _____ new.
6. That man is Yuri. _____ in my class.
7. Her name is Luz. _____ Puerto Rican.
8. My name is Yoko. _____ a Japanese name.

3. Write the possessive adjectives *my, your, his,* or *her*.

1. I have a book. __My__ book is in my backpack.
2. You have a paper. This is _____ paper.
3. He has a pen. _____ pen is on his desk.
4. She has a chair. This is _____ chair.
5. Hi! _____ name is George. I'm from Greece.
6. Who are you? What's _____ name?
7. He is Polish. _____ name is Marek.

4. Read the answers. Write questions. Use *Who, What,* or *Where*.

1. __Where is Brazil?_____ Brazil is in South America.
2. _____ He's a new student.
3. _____ The teacher is in the classroom.
4. _____ My name is Nydia.
5. _____ He is from Morocco.
6. _____ I'm from Japan.
7. _____ It's a computer disk.

5. Find the eight errors and correct them.

1. ~~I am~~ a new student in this class. *(I'm)*
2. You is in my class.
3. What is it your name?
4. This is Elena. she is my classmate.
5. Who's he from?
6. I from Syria.
7. Mr. Ives is the teacher. He a good teacher.
8. You,re a good student.

TEST YOURSELF ON CHAPTER 2

6. Write the plural.

1. a book   <u>books</u>
2. a computer   _____
3. a man   _____
4. an eraser   _____
5. a child   _____

6. a woman   _____
7. a key   _____
8. a picture   _____
9. a classmate   _____
10. a person   _____

7. Write *we, you, they* + the correct form of *be*. Use short forms.

1. Luis and I are Colombian. <u>We're</u> from Cali.
2. You and your brother are in my class. _____ my classmates.
3. These books are in English. _____ ESL books.
4. These two teachers are from Texas. _____ American.
5. My classmates and I are new here. _____ new students.
6. You, Marta, and Siok are in the same class. _____ classmates.

8. Write *There's* or *There are*.

1. <u>There's</u> a class in Room 215.
2. _____ 20 people in the class.
3. _____ windows in the classroom.

4. _____ a dictionary on the desk.
5. _____ a map on the wall.
6. _____ two wastebaskets in the room.

9. Write *this* or *these*.

1. <u>This</u> is a calculator.
2. What's _____ ?
3. _____ are our classmates.

4. What are _____ ?
5. _____ are CDs.
6. _____ is our classroom.

10. Find the eight errors and correct them.

      There are
1. ~~There's~~ eleven computers in this room.
2. Mikhail and I are from Moscow. We,re Russian.
3. These mens are from Indonesia.
4. The students they are in class.

5. What's these?
6. What are theirs names?
7. There is five children in my family.
8. Jad and Monta are from Thailand. There Thai.

See Answer Key pages ANS-1 and ANS-2.

At Home

Chapter 3

Families

- Negative statements with *be*
- *Yes/No* questions and short answers with *be*
- *Have* and *has*
- *How old* and *How many* questions

Chapter 4

Nice Eyes and a Great Smile

- The article *a/an*
- Descriptive adjectives (for example, *big, good, long*)
- *That/those*
- Possessive nouns (for example, *Jack's, the students'*)

GRAMMAR IN ACTION

Reading and Listening

A. Listen and read the conversation.

Irene: Diego, are you married?

Diego: Yes, I am. Here's a picture of my wife.

Irene: What's her name?

Diego: Carmen.

Irene: Do you have children?

Diego: Yes, I have two, one boy and one girl. Here's a picture of them.

Irene: How old are they?

Diego: My son, Manuel, is four years old, and my daughter, Luisa, is two.

Irene: You have a beautiful family.

Diego: Thank you.

B. Work with a partner. Practice the conversation in Part A.

Think about Grammar

A. Read the sentences. Then listen and circle the sentence you hear.

1. a. (Are you married?)　　　　　b. You are married.
2. a. Is this your wife?　　　　　　b. This is my wife.
3. a. Do you have children?　　　　b. You have children.
4. a. Is this your son?　　　　　　 b. This is my son.
5. a. How old is your son?　　　　 b. Who is your son?
6. a. Is this your daughter?　　　　b. This is my daughter.

B. Listen to Irene. Circle Diego's answers.

1. a. Yes, I am.　　　　　　　　　　b. I have two children.
2. a. Yes, I am.　　　　　　　　　　b. Yes, I have two.
3. a. It's a picture of my wife.　　　 b. They're my children.
4. a. He's four.　　　　　　　　　　 b. Manuel.
5. a. Yes, this is Luisa.　　　　　　　b. Two.
6. a. Thank you.　　　　　　　　　　b. No, it's not.

C. Mark your answers to the questions. Ask your partner the questions. Mark your partner's answers.

	YOU		YOUR PARTNER	
	YES	NO	YES	NO
1. Are you married?	❏	❏	❏	❏
2. Do you have children?	❏ How many? 1 2 3 _____	❏	❏ How many? 1 2 3 _____	❏
3. Do you have brothers?	❏ How many? 1 2 3 _____	❏	❏ How many? 1 2 3 _____	❏
4. Do you have sisters?	❏ How many? 1 2 3 _____	❏	❏ How many? 1 2 3 _____	❏

GRAMMAR BRIEFING 1

Negative Statements with *Be*

A. SINGULAR

FULL FORMS			
SUBJECT PRONOUN	BE	NOT	
I	am		
You	are		
He		not	old.
She	is		
It			

SHORT FORMS		
PRONOUN + BE	NOT	
I'm		
You're		
He's	not	old.
She's		
It's		

PRONOUN	BE + NOT	
—	—	
You	aren't	
He		old.
She	isn't	
It		

B. PLURAL

FULL FORMS			
SUBJECT PRONOUN	BE	NOT	
We			
You	are	not	old.
They			

SHORT FORMS		
PRONOUN + BE	NOT	
We're		
You're	not	old.
They're		

PRONOUN	BE + NOT	
We		
You	aren't	old.
They		

1. Short Forms → Full Forms

Write the full forms of *be + not*.

1. he's not = *he is not*
2. we're not = _____
3. she isn't = _____
4. he isn't = _____
5. I'm not = _____
6. it's not = _____
6. you aren't = _____
7. they aren't = _____
8. you're not = _____

2. Full Forms → Short Forms

Underline the subject and the full forms of *be + not*. Write the short forms.

She's not/She isn't
1. <u>She is not</u> in class.
2. They are not married.
3. It is not my book.
4. I am not a teacher.
5. We are not children.
6. He is not her husband.
7. You are not late.
8. She is not his wife.
9. They are not here today.

3. Using Short Forms of *Be* + *Not*

A. Complete. Use *be* + *not*. Write short forms.

A student ID (an identification card)

Irene: Look, there's a student ID on this desk. "Diego Salazar." Diego, is this your ID? Look.

Diego: My last name <u>isn't</u> "Salazar." It's "Alicea." I _____ from Venezuela, and my
       1   2

   eyes _____ blue. This _____ my picture!
        3   4

Irene: OK, OK! It _____ your ID! So, who's Diego Salazar?
              5

Diego: I don't know. He _____ in any of my classes.
                    6

B. Work with a partner. Practice the conversation in Part A.

C. These statements are false. Make them true. Use short forms of *be* + *not*.

Example   *Student A:* 1. Diego's last name is Salazar.
          Student B: No, Diego's last name **isn't** Salazar.

1. Diego's last name is Salazar.
2. He is from Venezuela.
3. His eyes are blue.
4. His picture is on the ID.

5. It's his ID.
6. These men are in the same classes.
7. They are friends.
8. Irene's ID is on the desk.

GRAMMAR BRIEFING 2

Questions and Answers with *Be*

A. *YES/NO* QUESTIONS

QUESTIONS			SHORT ANSWERS	
BE	SUBJECT		YES	NO
Am	I		Yes, I **am**.	No, **I'm not**.
	we		Yes, we **are**.	No, **we're not**./No, we **aren't**.
Are	you	in the picture?	Yes, you **are**.	No, **you're not**./No, you **aren't**.
	they		Yes, they **are**.	No, **they're not**./No, they **aren't**.
	he		Yes, he **is**.	No, **he's not**./No, he **isn't**.
Is	she		Yes, she **is**.	No, **she's not**./No, she **isn't**.
	it		Yes, it **is**.	No, **it's not**./No, it **isn't**.

B. *WH-* QUESTIONS WITH *HOW OLD*

QUESTIONS			ANSWERS
HOW OLD	BE	SUBJECT	
How old	**is**	she?	Two. OR She's two years old.
	are	they?	He's 30, and she's 25.

 Grammar Hotspot!

1. Use full forms after *Yes*.

   Q: Is she married?
   A: **Yes**, she **is**.
      NOT: Yes, ~~she's~~.

2. Use short forms after *No*.

   Q: Is he married?
   A: **No**, he **isn't**.
      NOT USUALLY: No, he is not.

4. *Yes/No Questions and Answers with Be + I/We*

Put the words in order. Write the questions and answers. Remember capital letters.

1. (beautiful/I/am/?)   (you/yes/are/./,)

2. *A:* _____   *B:* _____
   we/on the right bus/are/?   are/we/yes/./,

3. *A:* _____   *B:* _____
   late/I/am/?   no/aren't/you/./,

4. *A:* _____   *B:* _____
   in the right line/we/are/?   you're/no/not/./,

5. *Yes/No Questions and Answers with Be + You/He/She/It/They*

A. Complete the conversations.

1. *A:* __Are you_____ married?

   B: No, _____ . I'm single.

2. *A:* _____ he married?

   B: No, _____ . He's single.

3. *A:* _____ she from Japan?

   B: Yes, _____ .

4. *A:* Hi! _____ in this class?

   B: Yes, I _____ . I'm a new

   student.

5. *A:* Here's a pen. _____ your pen?

   B: Yes, it _____ . Thank you.

6. *A:* What a beautiful girl! _____ your sister?

   B: Yes, _____ .

7. *A:* _____ Friday?

   B: No, _____ . It's Thursday.

8. *A:* _____ from Colombia?

   B: No, _____ . They're from Mexico.

B. Work with a partner. Ask and answer the questions from Part A.

6. Questions with *How Old*

Ask and answer questions about the pictures. Use *How old.*

> Example   *Student A:* How old is she?
> *Student B:* I think she's 20.

7. Questions and Answers with *Be*

A. Read about the man in the picture.

 This is Yusef. He's from Kuwait. He's a student at Boston University. He's 21 years old. He's not married. He's single.

B. Write *yes/no* and *wh-* questions about Yusef. Write the answers.

1. Who's this?   This is Yusef.

2. Is he a student?   _____

3. How old is he?   _____

4. _____   _____

C. Write about the woman in the picture.

 This is _____

_____

_____

_____

D. Write about the couple in the picture.

This is a picture of _____ and _____

_____

_____

_____

E. Ask and answer questions about the people in C and D.

Example   *Student A:* Who's this?

   Student B: Her name is . . .

⭐ GRAMMAR BRIEFING 3

Present Tense of *Have*—Affirmative Statements

SUBJECT PRONOUN	VERB	
I		I **have** my books.
we	**have**	We **have** our books.
you		You **have** your books.
they		The students **have** their books.
he		The man **has** his car.
she	**has**	The woman **has** her car.
it		The car **has** a radio.

---

8. *Have vs. Has*

A. Circle *have* or *has*.

1. I (have/has) two brothers.

2. He (have/has) one sister.

3. They (have/has) no children.

4. She (have/has) a big family.

5. We (have/has) a small room.

6. Diego (have/has) a family.

B. Write *have* or *has*.

1. You _____ a good map.

2. It _____ nice pictures.

3. I _____ a long name.

4. You and I _____ long names.

5. My classmates _____ their books.

6. This room _____ no windows.

9. Using *Have* and *Has*

Work with a partner. Make true statements. Use the words in the boxes.

| I
You
We
The teacher
This room
Our classmates | + | have
has | + | a book/books
a pen/pens
a watch/watches
a clock/clocks
a window/windows
a car/cars | a desk/desks
a family/families
a picture/pictures
a backpack/backpacks
a blackboard/blackboards
_____ |

Example   *Student A:* I have a book.
          Student B: We have families.

10. Writing Statements with *Have* and *Has*

Complete the sentences on a piece of paper. Use *have* or *has*. Write true statements.

Example   I have five sisters.

1. I . . . .

2. My teacher . . . .

3. My classmates . . . .

4. We . . . .

5. Our classroom . . . .

6. I . . . .

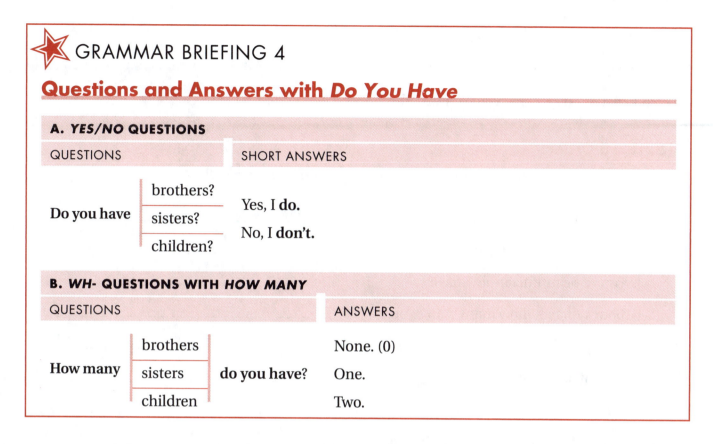

11. Forms of *Have* in Questions and Statements

Write *have* or *has*.

1. Do you ___have___ children?

2. How many brothers and sisters do you _____?

3. You _____ beautiful children.

4. She _____ no brothers or sisters.

5. Do you _____ a picture of your family?

6. Maria _____ a husband.

7. How many classmates do you _____?

8. Do you _____ a car?

9. The students _____ pictures of their families.

10. The classroom _____ pictures on the walls.

12. *Do You Have* Questions and Answers

Listen to the questions. Say your answer: *Yes, I do.* or *No, I don't.*

13. Word Order

Write a statement with a period (.) or a question with a question mark (?).

1. a nice picture / have / you / .   You have a nice picture.
2. you / have / do / sisters / ?   _____
3. you /a beautiful family / have / .   _____
4. books / have / how many / do / you / ?   _____
5. pictures / have / you / how many / do / ?   _____
6. a lot of papers / have / you / .   _____
7. do / have / you / children / ?   _____
8. have / do / you / how many / classes / ?   _____

14. Asking Questions with *Have*

A. Ask three students about their families. Ask questions with *Do you have* and *How many*. Complete the chart.

Example   *Student A:* Henri, do you have brothers?
          Student B: Yes, I do.
          Student A: How many brothers do you have?

Write names: Write numbers:

NAMES	BROTHERS	SISTERS	CHILDREN
1. _____			
2. _____			
3. _____			

B. On a piece of paper, write three sentences about one student and his or her family.

EXTRA PRACTICE

15. Negative Statements with *Be*

Write negative statements. Use the words in parentheses + *be* + *not*. Use short forms.

1. (he/my husband) He's not my husband./He isn't my husband. _____

2. (she/my wife) _____

3. (it/my ID) _____

4. (they/our children) _____

5. (you/21) _____

6. (we/married) _____

7. (I/hungry) _____

8. (these people/in this class) _____

16. *Yes/No* Questions and Short Answers with *Be*

Write *yes/no* questions. Use the words in parentheses + *be*. Complete the short answers.

1. (you/married) Are you married? _____ Yes, I am. _____

2. (Anna/your girlfriend) _____ Yes, _____

3. (Lin and Yoko/in your class) _____ No, _____

4. (you/our new teacher) _____ No, _____

5. (I/in this group) _____ Yes, _____

6. (we/in Room 211) _____ Yes, _____

7. (it/a nice day) _____ Yes, _____

17. Forms of *Have*

Write *have* or *has*.

1. Irene and David _____ dark hair.

2. David _____ nice eyes.

3. Diego and Carmen _____ children.

4. Diego _____ a mustache.

5. You _____ a great smile.

6. We _____ curly hair.

7. My name _____ 20 letters.

8. She _____ a short name.

18. Statements with *Have/Has*

A. Write statements. Use the subject in parentheses + *have* or *has* + (the picture).

   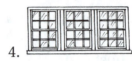

1.   2.   3.   4.   5.

1. (My brother) _My brother has a car._____

2. (We) _____

3. (The students) _____

4. (The classroom) _____

5. (The computer) _____

B. On a piece of paper, write five true statements about yourself and people in your family. Use *have* or *has*.

   Example   I have two sisters.

19. Questions with *Do You Have;* Short Answers

Put the words in order. Write the questions. Write your answers.

1. you/do/have/children _Do you have children?   Yes, I do. OR No, I don't._____

2. brothers/how many/have/you/do _____

3. have/you/do/a wife _____

4. have/you/sisters/do/how many _____

5. a boyfriend/you/have/do _____

6. you/do/have/classmates/how many _____

CHAPTER 4

Nice Eyes and a Great Smile

GRAMMAR IN ACTION

Reading and Listening

A. Listen and read the conversation.

Noriko: That's a good picture, Irene.

Diego: Is that your boyfriend?

Irene: No! It's my brother David.

Noriko: He's handsome.

Irene: I don't think so!

Noriko: Oh, yes, he is! He has nice eyes and a great smile.

Diego: Is he older or younger than you?

Irene: Younger. I'm 19, and he's 17. We have an older brother, too. He's 22.

Diego: What is that brother's name?

Irene: John. That's my father's name, too.

handsome = beautiful (Use *handsome* for boys and men. Use *beautiful* for girls and women, places, and things.)

B. Work in a group of three. Practice the conversation in Part A.

Think about Grammar

A. Find the correct sentence on page 55. Cross out the incorrect sentence.

1. a. That's **a good picture,** Irene.   b. ~~That's **good picture,** Irene.~~
2. a. He's **a handsome.**   b. He's **handsome.**
3. a. He has **a nice eyes.**   b. He has **nice eyes.**
4. a. He has **a great smile.**   b. He has **a smile great.**
5. a. Is he **older or younger** than you?   b. Is he **older and younger** than you?
6. a. We have **a older brother.**   b. We have **an older brother.**
7. a. It's **my father name,** too.   b. It's **my father's name,** too.

B. Listen to the questions about Irene and David. Circle your answers.

1. her boyfriend   (her brother)
2. Irene   David
3. Irene   David
4. 17   19
5. an older brother   an older sister
6. Yes, I think so.   No, I don't think so.
7. Yes, I think so.   No, I don't think so.

C. Look at the picture of this brother and sister. Take turns asking questions. For example, use *How old* and *Is he/she . . . .* Give your opinions with *Yes, I think so* or *No, I don't think so.*

Example   *Student A:* Is she beautiful?
           Student B: Yes, I think so.

GRAMMAR BRIEFING 1

The Article *A/An*

USING *A/AN* + NOUN

1. Use **the article *a* or *an*** before a singular noun.

> I have **a** pencil.
>
> I have **an** eraser.

2. Do not use *a* or *an* before a plural noun.

> She has pictures.
>   **NOT:** She has ~~a~~ pictures.

3. Use *a* before a consonant sound. Examples of consonant sounds are: /b/, /ch/, /k/, /d/, /f/, /g/, /h/, and /y/.

> **a b**ook, **a c**ar, **a d**esk, **a f**riend, **a h**andsome man, **a u**niversity

4. Use *an* before a vowel sound. Examples of vowel sounds are: /a/, /e/, /i/, /o/, and /u/.

> **an a**pple, **an e**nvelope, **an i**nch, **an o**ld friend, **an h**our, **an u**mbrella

 ## Grammar Hotspot!

Do not use *a* or *an* with a possessive adjective (for example, *my, your, his, her*).

> This is my pen.
>   **NOT:** This is ~~a~~ my pen.

1. *A* vs. *An*

Write the article *a* or *an*.

1. _*a*_ face

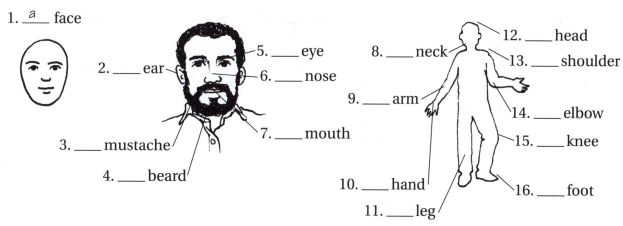

2. ___ ear

3. ___ mustache

4. ___ beard

5. ___ eye

6. ___ nose

7. ___ mouth

8. ___ neck

9. ___ arm

10. ___ hand

11. ___ leg

12. ___ head

13. ___ shoulder

14. ___ elbow

15. ___ knee

16. ___ foot

2. Using *A/An* or No Article

Student A: Point to body parts in the pictures for Exercise 1. Ask *What's this?* or *What are these?*
Student B: Answer with *a/an* (or no article for plural nouns). Take turns.

Example   *Student A (pointing):* What's this?
                   Student B: A face. What are these?
                   Student A: Legs.

3. *A/An* or No Article

Write *a, an,* or – (for no article).

A. I have __*a*__ nephew. He is _____ my sister's son. His _____ name is Boris. He's
       1   2   3

_____ handsome boy. Here's _____ picture of him. He has _____ nice eyes and
   4   5   6

_____ wonderful smile.
   7

B. This is _____ e-mail message from _____ my younger sister. She's in Taipei. She
                1   2

doesn't have _____ computer at home, but there are _____ computers at her school.
                      3   4

We have _____ older sister, too. She is _____ artist.
                5   6

C. Here's _____ my family tree. I have _____ big family. My relatives live in many
               1   2

different places. My _____ brother is in Cairo, and I have _____ sister in Istanbul.
                          3   4

I have _____ uncle in Paris and _____ aunt in Tokyo. I have _____ cousins in
             5   6   7

London and New York.

GRAMMAR BRIEFING 2

This, That, These, and *Those*

	SINGULAR	PLURAL

Things near the speaker:	**This** is my book.	**These** are my books.
Things **not** near the speaker:	Is **that** your book?	Are **those** your books?

A. WITH *BE*

SINGULAR

Use *this/that* + *is*.

> **This is** my friend Luis.
>
> **That is/That's** his brother.

PLURAL

Use *these/those* + *are*.

> **These are** old books.
>
> **Those are** new.

B. WITH NOUNS

SINGULAR

Use *this/that* + singular noun.

> He's in **this class.**
>
> Is **that boy** your son?

PLURAL

Use *these/those* + plural noun.

> **These glasses** are Maria's.
>
> Do you have **those papers?**

4. *That* vs. *Those*

Write *that* or *those*.

1. *A:* Is __that__ your pen?

   B: No, it's not.

2. *A:* Are _____ your books?

   B: No, they aren't.

3. *A:* Is _____ your paper?

   B: Yes, it is.

4. *A:* Are _____ new glasses?

   B: Yes, they are.

5. _____ desk is the teacher's.

6. _____ are Janet's pencils.

7. _____ women are in my class.

8. _____ is a picture of my family.

5. Writing Statements and Questions with *This/That/These/Those*

Write a question (a) and a statement (b) for each picture. Use *this, that, these,* or *those*.

1.

<u>Is this your CD?</u>
       a

<u>This CD is new.</u>
       b

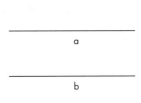

2.

_____
       a

_____
       b

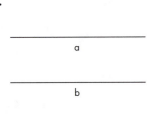

3.

_____
       a

_____
       b

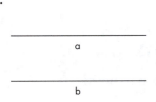

4.

_____
       a

_____
       b

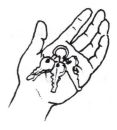

5.

_____
       a

_____
       b

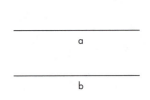

6.

_____
       a

_____
       b

6. Using *That* and *Those*

Student A: Point to parts of your body. Student B: Say *That's your . . .* or *Those are your . . .*
Take turns.

 GRAMMAR BRIEFING 3

Descriptive Adjectives

short hair

long hair

A. *BE* + ADJECTIVE	
Use *am/is/are* + adjective.	Her hair **is short.**
	Their hair **is long.**

B. ADJECTIVE + NOUN	
Use adjective + noun.	She has **short hair.**
	They have **long hair.**

 Grammar Hotspot!

Adjectives have one form. Do not add -*s* to an adjective.	He is tall, and he has tall brothers.
	NOT: He has tall*s* brothers.

7. Meanings of Adjectives

Ask and answer questions with adjectives. Take turns.

Example   *Student A:* Is Phil's hand large or small?
          Student B: It's large. Is the baby's hand large or small?
          Student A: It's small.

| large | small | happy | sad |

Phil's hand   the baby's hand   Bob   Walter

1. Is Phil's hand large or small?   4. Is Bob happy or sad?

| light | dark | heavy | thin |

Joe   Tom   Mike   Jeff

2. Is Joe's hair light or dark?   5. Is Mike heavy or thin?

| curly | straight | tall | short |

Paola   Jane   Tina   Hannah

3. Is Paola's hair curly or straight?   6. Is Tina tall or short?

8. Using Adjectives

Ask and answer questions with adjectives. Follow the example. Take turns.

> Example   *Student A:* Is this room big or little?
>   *Student B:* It's big.

1. this room: big—little
2. our school: big— little
3. our class: large—small
4. your family: large—small
5. the teacher: tall—short
6. the teacher: young—old

7. the teacher: married—single
8. _____ : married—single
   a classmate
9. _____ : tall—short
   a classmate
10. _____ : happy—sad
    a classmate

9. Words for Describing People, Places, and Things

A. Work in a group. Make a list of adjectives. You have one minute. Write fast!

B. Share the lists of adjectives from all the groups in the class.
Ask about new words: *What does . . . mean?*

C. On a piece of paper, write eight true sentences about yourself and other people. Use *be* + adjective or adjective + noun.

> Examples   Mahmoud is handsome.
>   I have dark eyes.

GRAMMAR BRIEFING 4

Possessive Nouns

THIS IS MY FRIEND JAE YONG.

Jae Yong   Javier

Javier has a friend. Jae Yong is **Javier's** friend.

A. SINGULAR NOUNS

Add **'s** to singular nouns.
  ' = an apostrophe.

That boy has a dog. It is the **boy's** dog.

Mr. Hall has a son. He is Mr. **Hall's** son.

B. REGULAR PLURAL NOUNS

Add only **'** to plural nouns ending in -s.

Those boys have a dog. It is the **boys'** dog.

The Halls have a son. He is the **Halls'** son.

C. IRREGULAR PLURAL NOUNS (NO -S)

Add **'s** to irregular plural nouns.

The men have wives. They are the **men's** wives.

People have names. What are those **people's** names?

  ## Grammar Hotspot!

Sometimes **'s** means *is*. Sometimes **'s** is possessive.

It + is   *possessive*
  It**'s** the children**'s** dog.

10. Singular and Plural Possessive Nouns

Complete the sentences. Use possessive nouns.

1. Javier has a sister. She's _Javier's_ sister.

2. The boys have a mother. She's the _____ mother.

3. The girl has a cat. It's the _____ cat.

4. Ali has two daughters. They're _____ daughters.

5. Her children have friends. They're her _____ friends.

6. Tony has a girlfriend. She's _____ girlfriend.

7. His sisters have boyfriends. They're his _____ boyfriends.

8. The girls have a father. He's the _____ father.

9. The teacher has a desk. It's the _____ desk.

10. The students have a classroom. It's the _____ classroom.

11. Statements with Possessive Nouns

A. Read the two sentences. Write one sentence with the same meaning. Use a possessive noun.

1. My father has a store. It's in the city. _My father's store is in the city._ _____

2. My parents have a house. It's white. _____

3. My aunt has a baby. He's one month old. _____

4. My cousins have a school. It's in California. _____

5. My brother has a car. It's Japanese. _____

6. My sisters have a bedroom. It's nice. _____

7. My uncle has a job. It's at a bank. _____

8. My grandfather has dogs. They're friendly. _____

B. On a piece of paper, write six true statements about people in your family. Use singular and plural possessive nouns.

Examples   My mother's name is Myung Soon.

My grandparents' house is small.

12. Using Possessive Nouns

A. Student A: Ask questions with *Who*. Use the **boldfaced** words in your question.
Student B: Look at Diego's family tree. Listen and answer the questions.

Example   *Student A:* Who's Juan?

Student B: Juan is Diego's father.

1. **Juan** is ___Diego's___ father.

2. **Carmen** is _____ wife.

3. _____ is **Diego and Carmen's son.**

4. _____ is **Manuel's sister.**

5. **Diego and Carmen** are Manuel and

   _____ parents.

6. **Maria** is Luisa and _____

   grandmother.

B. Student B: Ask questions with *Who*.
Student A: Listen and answer.

Example   *Student B:* Who's Carla?

Student A: Carla is Diego's sister.

1. **Carla** is ___Diego's___ sister.

2. **Roberto** is _____ husband.

3. _____ is **Carla and Roberto's**

   daughter.

4. _____ are **Bella's cousins.**

5. **Carla and Roberto** are Manuel and

   _____ aunt and uncle.

6. _____ is **Diego's brother-in-law.**

C. Keep working with your partner. Ask and answer more questions about Diego's family.

Example   *Student A:* Who is Bella's uncle?

EXTRA PRACTICE

13. Using *A, An,* or − (no article)

Write *a, an,* or − (for no article).

Vitek has __a__ big family. He has _____ five brothers and _____ sister. He has
                 1   2   3

_____ aunts, uncles, and cousins, too. They live in many different places. Vitek has
   4

_____ older brother in London. He is _____ doctor. Vitek has _____ younger
   5   6   7

brothers in the Czech Republic. They live with _____ their mother and father. His
                                                   8

younger brothers are _____ students. _____ Vitek's sister is in New York. She is
                        9   10

_____ artist. He has _____ aunt and _____ uncle in France. They have _____
  11   12   13   14

school in Paris. He has _____ aunts, uncles, and cousins in Venezuela, too.
                          15

14. *That* vs. *Those*

Write *that* or *those.*

1. Is _____ a picture of your girlfriend?

2. Is _____ Irene's boyfriend?

3. Are _____ Julia's children?

4. Are _____ books the teacher's?

5. Is _____ paper Nilda's?

6. Are _____ men your uncles?

15. *This, That, These, Those*

On a piece of paper, write a statement and a question about each picture. Use *this, that, these,* and *those.*

1.    2.    3. 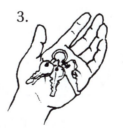   4.

Example That is my car.

16. Descriptive Adjectives

Put the words in order. Write statements. Circle the adjectives.

1. Paola/hair/curly/has _Paola has (curly) hair._

2. light/Joe's/hair/is _____

3. are/Tom's/blue/eyes _____

4. large/are/Phil's/hands _____

5. eyes/brown/has/Jane _____

6. have/they/hair/long _____

17. Descriptive Adjectives

What do you look like? Complete the four statements. Write them on a piece of paper. Use descriptive adjectives.

1. My hair . . . .

2. My eyes . . . .

3. I have . . . .

4. My/I . . . .

Example My hair is short and brown.

18. Possessive Nouns

Complete the sentences. Use possessive nouns.

1. Khaled has a daughter. She is _Khaled's_ daughter.

2. The boy has a sister. She is the _____ sister.

3. The boys have a father. He is the _____ father.

4. Jane has a boyfriend. He is _____ boyfriend.

5. My parents have a house. It is my _____ house.

6. Her children have a cat. It is her _____ cat.

7. Tony has a bicycle. It is _____ bicycle.

8. My sisters have children. They are my _____ children.

Unit 2 Wrap-Up Activities

1. My Friend Noha: READING

Read this student's paragraph.

> I have a friend at school. Her name is Noha. She's from Kuwait. She's 19 years old. She's not married. She has dark eyes and dark hair. Her hair is long. She's not tall or short. She's average height. She's a good friend.

2. Someone You Know: WRITING

On a piece of paper, write about a friend or a person in your family. Who is it? What does he or she look like?

3. My Friend Alicia: EDITING

Find and correct the ten errors. The first one is corrected for you.

> My ~~friends'~~ friend's name is Alicia Vasquez. She is friend in a my class. She is a pretty. She has hair long and browns eyes. She no is tall. She is average height. Alicias family is in the Dominican Republic. She have a parents, two brothers, and one sister at home.

4. Talking about a Family: SPEAKING/LISTENING

This is Lisa's family. Who are the people in the picture? Talk about them with a partner.

Example   *Student A:* This is Lisa's husband.

                Student B: I don't think so. He's old. That's Lisa's father.

Lisa Kalmar

5. Your Family: SPEAKING/LISTENING

Work with a partner. Show a photo of your family, or draw your family tree. (For example, see Diego's family tree on page 66.) Tell your partner about the people in your family. Ask four or more questions about your partner's family.

GRAMMAR SUMMARY

The Verb *Be*

NEGATIVE STATEMENTS

FULL FORMS		CONTRACTIONS			
I	**am not** hungry.	I**'m not**	hungry.	—	
He		He**'s not**		He	
She	**is not** here.	She**'s not**	here.	She	**isn't** here.
It		It**'s not**		It	
We		We**'re not**		We	
You	**are not** late.	You**'re not**	late.	You	**aren't** late.
They		They**'re not**		They	

YES/NO QUESTIONS

QUESTIONS	SHORT ANSWERS
Am I late?	Yes, I **am.**
	No, I**'m not.**
Is he/she/it here?	Yes, he/she/it **is.**
	No, he/she/it**'s not./isn't.**
Are we/you/they late?	Yes, we/you/they **are.**
	No, we/you/they**'re not./aren't.**

QUESTIONS WITH *HOW OLD*

How old are they?

How old is he/she/it?

★ See the Grammar Briefings on pages 44 and 46.

Articles

She has **a** younger sister and **an** older brother.

Do you have [0] cousins?

★ See the Grammar Briefing on page 57.

The Verb *Have*

AFFIRMATIVE STATEMENTS

I	
You	
We	**have** short hair.
They	
He	
She	**has** long legs.
It	

YES/NO QUESTIONS	ANSWERS
Do you have brothers?	Yes, I **do.**
	No, I **don't.**
How many brothers **do you have?**	Two.

★ See the Grammar Briefings on pages 49 and 51.

This, That, These, and *Those*

SINGULAR	PLURAL
Is **this** your book?	**These** are my glasses.
Is **that** your pen?	**Those** glasses are John's.

★ See the Grammar Briefing on page 59.

Descriptive Adjectives

Your brother is **handsome.**

He has **nice** eyes.

★ See the Grammar Briefing on page 61.

Possessive Nouns

That is **Oscar's** car.

What are the **students'** names?

The **men's** room is here.

★ See the Grammar Briefing on page 64.

TEST YOURSELF ON CHAPTER 3

1. Complete the statements. Use forms of *be* + *not*. Use short forms.

   1. I __'m not__ from this city.
   2. He _____ married.
   3. We _____ in the same class.

   4. This classroom _____ large.
   5. Those boys _____ brothers.
   6. You _____ late.

2. Complete each *yes/no* question and short answer.

   1. *A:* __Are you__ hungry?
      B: No, I _____ .
   2. *A:* _____ a long movie?
      B: Yes, it _____ .
   3. *A:* _____ married?
      B: No, they _____ .

   4. *A:* _____ her brother?
      B: Yes, he _____ .
   5. *A:* _____ late?
      B: No, we _____ .
   6. *A:* _____ cold?
      B: Yes, I _____ .

3. Write *have* or *has*.

   1. I __have__ no children.
   2. My sister _____ two children.
   3. We _____ new watches.

   4. Diego _____ a mustache.
   5. Esperanza _____ a long name.
   6. You _____ a big family.

4. Put the words in order. Write questions.

   1. in school / they / are _Are they in school?_____
   2. how many / brothers / you / have / do _____
   3. you / have / sisters / do _____
   4. he / how old / is _____
   5. children / you / have / how many / do _____

5. Find the six errors and correct them.

   1. Do you have brothers? Yes, I ~~am~~. *do*
   2. How old she is?
   3. You has a nice car.
   4. Do you has children?
   5. She no is married.
   6. Is he handsome? Yes, he's.

TEST YOURSELF ON CHAPTER 4

6. Write *a, an,* or − (for no article).

1. Irene has <u>a</u> brother.

2. She has _____ picture of her brother.

3. It's _____ excellent picture.

4. Irene's brother has _____ nice smile.

5. She has _____ pictures of her parents.

6. Bob is _____ happy man.

7. He has _____ two children.

8. They have _____ old house.

7. Write *that* or *those.*

1. <u>That</u> is your paper.

2. Are _____ your pens?

3. _____ are my books.

4. Is _____ his wife?

5. _____ ID isn't Diego's.

6. _____ keys aren't Ali's.

8. Put the words in order. Write statements.

1. she / hair / long / has <u>She has long hair.</u>

2. Phil's / small / car / is _____

3. blue / his / eyes / are _____

4. that / a / good / is / picture _____

9. Write the possessive form of the noun in parentheses ( ).

1. (teacher) Those are the <u>teacher's</u> books.

2. (Mary) Those are _____ sisters.

3. (brothers) What are his _____ names?

4. (people) I have two _____ papers.

5. (friend) That's my _____ wife.

6. (parents) That is her _____ car.

10. Find the eight errors and correct them.

1. Irene has ~~an~~ younger brother.

2. They're handsomes boys.

3. Those are Mr. Hall keys.

4. Here's picture of my family.

5. That's my friends Pavel and Eva.

6. He's a boy tall.

7. That is her husbands' car.

8. Those girls have a cat. It's the girl's cat.

See Answer Key pages ANS-2 and ANS-3.

Busy People

Chapter 5
What Are You Doing?

- Present progressive tense, affirmative statements
- Spelling of *–ing* verbs
- Present progressive questions
- More about plural nouns

Chapter 6
What About You?

- Negative statements in the present progressive
- Affirmative and negative statements with *can*
- *Yes/No* questions and answers with *can*
- The conjunctions *and, but,* and *or*

CHAPTER

5

What Are You Doing?

GRAMMAR IN ACTION

Reading and Listening

A. Listen and read.

Narrator: It's 6:00 on Monday evening. Oscar and Susan are at home. They're in the kitchen, and the radio is playing. Oscar is sitting at the table. He's holding the baby. They're having supper. (*Ring!*) The phone is ringing. Listen to the conversation.

Susan: Hello?

Brian: Hi, Susan!

Susan: Oh, hi, Brian! How are you?

Brian: I'm fine, thanks. Listen, what are you doing? Is this a good time to talk, or are you busy? I'm calling about the party for Mom and Dad.

Susan: Well, we're eating right now.

Brian: OK, you're busy! So, I'll call back. Say hi to Oscar.

Susan: OK. I'll talk to you later.

Brian: Bye!

Susan: Bye-bye.

B. Work with a partner. Practice the conversation in Part A.

Think about Grammar

A. Write *eating, sitting, ringing,* or *talking.*

1. She's <u>talking</u> .   2. They're _____ .   3. It's _____ .   4. He's _____ .

B. Make sentences about the story on page 76. Student A: Say the first part of a sentence. Student B: Find and say the second part. Take turns.

Example   *Student A:* 1. Susan and Oscar . . .
    Student B: . . . are having supper.   2. The phone . . .

FIRST PART:	SECOND PART:
1. Susan and Oscar . . .	a. is ringing.
2. The phone . . .	b. are having supper.
3. Susan and Brian . . .	c. is holding the baby.
4. Oscar . . .	d. is playing.
5. The baby . . .	e. are talking on the phone.
6. Oscar and the baby . . .	f. is smiling.
7. The radio . . .	g. are sitting at the table.

C. How do you spell the *-ing* verb?

FIND IT IN THE CONVERSATION.	CAN YOU GUESS?
1. a. ring + -ing <u>ringing</u> b. talk + -ing _____	c. work + -ing _____
2. a. smile + -ing _____ b. have + -ing _____	c. write + -ing _____
3. a. sit + -ing _____	b. stop + -ing _____

GRAMMAR BRIEFING 1

Present Progressive Tense*—Affirmative Statements

A. SINGULAR

FULL FORMS			CONTRACTIONS†	
SUBJECT	*BE*	BASE VERB + *-ING*	SUBJECT + *BE*	BASE VERB + *-ING*
I	am		I'm	
You	are		You're	
He		working.	He's	working.
She	is		She's	
It			It's	

B. PLURAL

FULL FORMS			CONTRACTIONS†	
SUBJECT	*BE*	BASE VERB + *-ING*	SUBJECT + *BE*	BASE VERB + *-ING*
We			We're	
You	are	working.	You're	working.
They			They're	

*Another name for the present progressive tense is **present continuous.**

†**Contractions** = short forms.

 Grammar Hotspot!

1. Use the present progressive for actions happening now, at this moment.

> Susan is on the phone right now.
>   She **is talking.**

2. Remember! Use a form of *be* with the *-ing* verb.

> **I'm** talking to Brian.
>   NOT: ~~I talking~~ to Brian.

1. Verb Meanings

A. Match the pictures and the statements.

Example   *Student A:* Picture number 1 is b, It's playing.

a. She's thinking.

d. He's studying.

g. They're swimming.

b. It's playing.

e. It's sleeping.

h. It's raining.

c. They're drinking.

f. She's cooking.

i. He's running.

B. Work with a partner. Cover the words in Part A. Say what is happening in each picture.

2. Present Progressive Statements with *I* and *We*

A. What are you doing? Check (✓) your answers.

	YOU	YOUR PARTNER
1. I'm doing Exercise 2.	✓	
2. I'm sitting in class.		
3. I'm reading.		
4. I'm writing with a pen.		
5. I'm writing with a pencil.		
6. I'm listening to music.		
7. I'm working with a partner.		
8. I'm holding a book.		
9. I'm thinking about lunch.		
10. I'm learning English.		

B. Work with a partner. Ask *What are you doing?* Check (✓) your partner's answers.

C. Write about you and your partner. What are both of you doing?

1. We're _____

2. _____

3. _____

3. Present Progressive Statements

Work with your class. Take turns doing something. Watch your classmates and answer the teacher's questions.

Example   *Teacher:* What's she doing?

Students: She's washing her hair.

Teacher: What are they doing?

Students: They're dancing.

GRAMMAR BRIEFING 2

Spelling *-ing* Verb Forms

SPELLING RULES*

1. Most verbs: Add *-ing* to the **base form of the verb.**	go → going carry → carrying wear → wearing sleep → sleeping
2. Verbs that end in *ie:* Change the *ie* to *y,* and add *-ing*.	lie → lying die → dying
3. Verbs that end in a consonant† + *e:* Drop the *e,* and add *-ing*.	write → writing take → taking

*See Appendix 5 for more on spelling *-ing* verb forms.
†See page 2 for lists of consonants and vowels.

Grammar Hotspot!

To spell most verbs that end in "C V C" (consonant + vowel + consonant): Double the final consonant and add *-ing*.	cut → cutting begin → beginning

4. Spelling Base Verb Forms

Write the base form of each verb.

1. living   _live_   4. putting _____   7. playing _____

2. speaking _____   5. lying _____   8. taking _____

3. asking _____   6. beginning _____   9. pointing _____

5. Spelling *-ing* Verb Forms

A. Write the *-ing* form of each verb.

1. fix   _fixing_   5. give _____   9. say _____

2. go _____   6. make _____   10. stop _____

3. sing _____   7. ride _____   11. get _____

4. run _____   8. die _____   12. do _____

B. Complete the statements. Use *-ing* verbs from Part A.

1.

She's _____ the mail.

3.

She's _____ a bike.

2.

They're _____ the car.

4.

He's _____ coffee.

6. Asking about Verb Meanings

Look at the verbs in Exercises 4 and 5. Ask your teacher about the meanings of new words.

Example   *Student A:* What does sing mean?
             Teacher:

7. Present Progressive, Full Forms

Complete the sentences. Use the present progressive. Write full forms, not contractions.

I __am sitting__ in my classroom with my classmates. We _____ for
    1. sit   2. wait

the teacher. Yusuke _____ a book. Some people _____ their
                        3. read   4. do

homework. Aida and Carol _____ . They _____ Chinese,
                              5. talk   6. speak

I think. I _____ Oscar and Juan. They _____
          7. watch   8. stand

by the window. Viktor and Pavel _____ to music. They
                                   9. listen

_____ headphones, so I can't hear it. What are they
  10. wear

listening to?

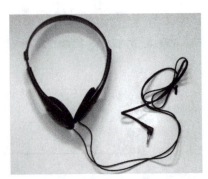

Headphones

GRAMMAR BRIEFING 3

Present Progressive Questions

A. *YES/NO QUESTIONS AND SHORT ANSWERS*

QUESTIONS			SHORT ANSWERS	
BE	SUBJECT	BASE VERB + -ING	YES	NO
Am	I		Yes, I **am**.	No, I**'m not**.
	we		Yes, we **are**.	No, we**'re not**/we **aren't**.
Are	you	win**ning**?	Yes, you **are**.	No, you**'re not**/you **aren't**.
	they		Yes, they **are**.	No, they**'re not**/they **aren't**.
	he		Yes, he **is**.	No, he**'s not**/he **isn't**.
Is	she		Yes, she **is**.	No, she**'s not**/she **isn't**.
	it		Yes, it **is**.	No, it**'s not**/it **isn't**.

B. QUESTIONS AND ANSWERS WITH *WHAT*

QUESTIONS				ANSWERS
WHAT	BE	SUBJECT	BASE VERB + -*ING*	
What	**are**	you	watch**ing**?	An old movie.
		he		
	is	she	**doing**?	Making coffee.
		it		

💬 **Talking the Talk**

Use the contraction *What's* in conversation.

WRITE	SAY
What is he wearing?	**What's** he wearing?

8. Forming *Yes/No Questions*

A. Read two e-mail messages to David, a college student. Complete the *yes/no* questions.

From: jennarose@newtoncoll.edu (Jenna Hillhouse)

To: d_hillhouse@southstate.edu (David Hillhouse)

Hey Little Brother! How are you? <u>Are things going</u> _____ well for you at
                  1. things/go

school? I hope everything's OK! _____ a lot? I'm taking 4 hard
               2. you/study

courses this semester. It's no fun. How's your room? _____ OK?
         3. you and your roommate/get along

I'm living with Lisa this year. We have a pretty nice room. _____
             4. the sun/shine

there? It's cold and cloudy here. Well, back to work. Write to me! Love, Jenna

---

From: hillfamily@globalnet.com (Jerry and Diane Hillhouse)

To: d_hillhouse@southstate.edu (David Hillhouse)

Dear David,

How are you? _____ well at school? I hope so. And I hope you're
         5. things/go

taking care of yourself. _____ well? _____
       6. you/eat   7. you/get

enough sleep? Don't drink too much coffee! _____ your vitamins?
           8. you/take

_____ too many questions? (You know I worry about you!)
   9. I/ask

Dad's on the phone. He's calling your sister. _____ to you these
           10. Jenna/write

days? We miss you both!

Love, Mom

P. S. Dad says "Hello" and "Work hard!"

B. Write an e-mail message to a classmate or your teacher. Ask two or more *yes/no* questions in the present progressive tense.

From:
To:

9. Yes/No Questions and Short Answers

A. Student A: Look at the picture on page 76. Listen to the questions. Give short answers. Student B: Ask *yes/no* questions in the present progressive.

> Example   *Student B:* Are the people having dinner?
> *Student A:* Yes, they are.

1. the people/have dinner
2. they/watch TV
3. the woman/talk on the phone
4. she/drink coffee
5. the man/sit at the table
6. he/wear a jacket and tie
7. the radio/play
8. you/look at page 20

B. Student B: Look at the picture on page 90. Listen and give short answers. Student A: Ask the questions in the present progressive.

> Example   *Student A:* Is the man sitting down?
> *Student B:* Yes, he is.

1. the man/sit down
2. he/watch TV
3. he/hold his baby
4. his wife/watch TV with him
5. the TV/work
6. the cats/play
7. they/sleep
8. you/look at page 10

10. Asking and Answering Questions with *What*

A. Ask and answer questions about the pictures. Use *What* + these three verbs: *do, hold, wear.* Use the present progressive. Take turns.

Example *Student A:* What's he doing?

Student B: He's walking to work. What's he wearing?

B. Write three or more sentences to describe each picture. Write them on a piece of paper.

Picture 1: There's a man in the picture. He's going . . . .

Picture 2: There's a girl in the picture. She's . . . .

Picture 3: There are . . . .

11. Questions and Answers about What's Happening

A. Look at the picture. Take turns asking *wh-* questions about Oscar, Susan, and the other people at the party.

Example   *Student A:* Where's Oscar?

Student B: He's in the living room. What's he doing?

Student A: He's talking with a friend. Who's in the kitchen?

B. Write eight or more sentences about the picture. Use verbs in the present progressive.

Example   Oscar and Susan are having a party. Susan is in the kitchen. She's . . . .

GRAMMAR BRIEFING 4

More About Plural Nouns

A. SPELLING OF PLURAL NOUNS

1. Most nouns:
   Add -*s*.

student → students	radio → radios
day → days	shoe → shoes

2. Nouns ending in *ch, sh, ss,* or *x:*
   Add -*es*.

watch → watches	dish → dishes
class → classes	box → boxes

3. Nouns ending in a consonant + *y:*
   Drop the *y* and add -*ies*.

family → families
dictionary → dictionaries

4. Some nouns ending in *f* or *fe:*
   Drop the *f* or *fe* and add -*ves*.

wife → wives	knife → knives
leaf → leaves	loaf → loaves

See Appendix 3 for more information on the spelling of plural forms.

B. COUNT AND NONCOUNT NOUNS

1. Nouns with singular and plural forms are **count nouns.** You can count them.

> one student, two students, three . . . .

2. Some nouns are **noncount nouns.** Those nouns do not have singular and plural forms.

> I have **money**.
>   NOT: I have moneys.

See Chapter 10 for more information on nouns.

 Grammar Hotspot!

1. Some nouns have an irregular plural form.

> one foot, two **feet**
>
> one tooth, two **teeth**
>
> one person, two **people**

2. Some nouns have only a plural form (no singular).

> **clothes, pants, jeans, shorts, (eye)glasses, sunglasses**

12. Spelling Plural Nouns

Write the plural forms of these nouns.

1. class   *classes*
2. friend _____
3. family _____
4. wife   _____
5. tie   _____

6. office _____
7. key   _____
8. box   _____
9. knife   _____
10. foot   _____

11. baby   _____
12. tax   _____
13. desk   _____
14. brush _____
15. leaf   _____

13. Singular → Plural

Make these sentences plural.

1. That is his wife. *Those are their wives.* _____

2. This watch isn't working. _____

3. That dish is dirty. _____

4. Our class isn't big. _____

5. Your tooth is white. _____

6. The leaf on the tree is green. _____

7. The baby is crying. _____

8. This dictionary is heavy. _____

9. He's washing his foot. _____

10. The dress in that picture is pretty. _____

💬 Talking the Talk

Sometimes the *-(e)s* on a plural noun adds a syllable, for example:

•   • •

one house, two houses

House has one syllable; *houses* has two syllables.

Listen: one hairbrush, two hairbrushes.

Hairbrush has two syllables; *hairbrushes* has three syllables.

Listen again: lunch, lunches   face, faces   message, messages   box, boxes

14. Singular *vs.* Plural Nouns; Pronunciation of Plural Nouns

A. Circle the correct nouns.

It's Saturday afternoon. Oscar is at home.

He's sitting on the (couch/couches) in
                              1

the living room. His (cat/cats) are on the
                          2

couch, too. They're both sleeping. Oscar is wearing comfortable (clothe/clothes): a
                                                                                  3

(T-shirt/T-shirts), (jean/jeans), and (sock/socks) on his (foot/feet). There's a (TV/TVs)
        4   5   6   7   8

in the room, and Oscar is watching baseball. He has (thing/things) to eat on a
                                                          9

(table/tables). He has two (sandwich/sandwiches), a bowl of potato (chip/chips), and
     10   11   12

a big (glass/glasses) of Coke. He has an (apple/apples) and two (piece/pieces) of
        13   14   15

chocolate cake. He's ready for a long (afternoon/afternoons).
                                              16

B. Review your answers to Part A with a partner. Then look at the nouns in the chart. Check (✓) your answers.

DO YOU ADD A SYLLABLE ON THE PLURAL NOUN?	YES	NO
1. couches	✓	
2. cats		✓
3. socks		
4. tables		
5. sandwiches		
6. chips		
7. glasses		
8. pieces		

🎧

C. Listen and check your answers to Parts A and B. Practice saying the nouns in Part B with your partner.

EXTRA PRACTICE

15. Present Progressive Statements with Full Forms

Use the verbs under the lines in the present progressive. Write full forms.

It's almost 9:00 a.m. I am at my desk in class. I _____ with Fatima.
                                                          1. sit

She _____ a letter. Some people _____ their homework.
         2. write   3. do

We _____ for the teacher. Oscar and Juan are by the window. Oscar
        4. wait

_____ a little boy outside. The boy _____ to ride a bike.
        5. watch   6. learn

Juan _____ at a group of girls. They _____ soccer. Now
            7. look   8. play

the teacher _____ into the room. It's 9:00. The class _____.
                    9. come   10. begin

16. Present Progressive Statements with Contractions

Complete the statements in the present progressive. Use contractions.

1. (he/work) He's working _____ today.   5. (you/smile) _____.

2. (she/run) _____ .   6. (I/study) _____ English.

3. (it/stop) _____ .   7. (we/do) _____

4. (they/swim) _____ .   Exercise 16.

17. Questions and Answers in the Present Progressive

Match the questions and answers.

_____1. What are you doing?   a. Yes, I am.

_____2. Are you watching a movie?   b. The newspaper.

_____3. Is Ted watching TV?   c. He's reading.

_____4. What's Ted doing?   d. Watching TV.

_____5. What's he reading?   e. No, he isn't.

18. *Yes/No* Questions and Answers in the Present Progressive

Write *yes/no* questions in the present progressive. Complete the short answers.

1. (you/listen) __Are you listening?_____ Yes, __I am._____

2. (classes/start) _____ Yes, _____

3. (the woman/cry) _____ No, _____

4. (he/fix his car) _____ Yes, _____

5. (the bus/stop) _____ Yes, _____

6. (you/eat/now) _____ No, _____

19. Present Progressive Questions with *What*

Write questions with *What* + present progressive. Write answers.

1. _____

_____

2. _____

_____

3. _____

_____

20. Spelling Plural Count Nouns

Write the plural form of each noun.

1. box _____   6. library _____   11. lunch _____

2. family _____   7. day _____   12. house _____

3. television _____   8. kiss _____   13. suit _____

4. tooth _____   9. party _____   14. glass _____

5. knife _____   10. foot _____   15. watch _____

CHAPTER 6 What About You?

GRAMMAR IN ACTION

Reading and Listening

Vitaly, Idelia, and Oscar can't go to school today.

Vitaly isn't feeling well.
He's staying in bed.

Idelia's children aren't in school.
today. She's staying at home.

Oscar's car isn't running.
He's working on it.

A. Listen and read.

Narrator: It's Tuesday morning at 9:00. The teacher, Mr. Allen, is beginning his class. Some students aren't in class today. They're absent. Mr. Allen is asking about them.

Mr. Allen: Where's Miho? Is she absent today?

Miho: No, I'm here!

Mr. Allen: Oh, good morning, Miho. Let's see . . . Vitaly isn't here. Is he in school today?

Katya: No, he isn't. He's not feeling well.

Mr. Allen: I'm sorry to hear that. What about Idelia? Is she sick, too?

Miho: She's not sick, but she can't come today. Her children don't have school, and she's staying home with them.

Mr. Allen: Oh, that's too bad.

Katya: I can give her the homework.

Mr. Allen: Can you do that? Good. And what about Oscar? He's absent, too.

Juan: Oscar can't come today. His car isn't running.

Mr. Allen: That's too bad! Well, we have a small class today.

B. Form a group of 3–5 students. Practice the conversation in Part A.

Think about Grammar

A. Complete these negative statements from the conversation.

1. *Narrator:* Some students _aren't_ in class today.

2. *Katya:* No, he isn't. _____ feeling well.

3. *Miho:* _____ sick, but _____ today.

4. *Juan:* Oscar _____ today.

5. *Juan:* His car _____ .

B. Put the words in order. Write statements and questions from the conversation.

1. *Narrator:* asking/Mr. Allen/them/about/is .   _Mr. Allen is asking about them._

2. *Mr. Allen:* absent/today/she/is/?   _____

2. *Mr. Allen:* about/what/Idelia/?   _____

3. *Katya:* can/I/her/give/the/homework/.   _____

4. *Mr. Allen:* do/you/that/can/?   _____

5. *Mr. Allen:* Oscar/what/and/about/?   _____

C. Student A: Tell a problem. Students B and C: Respond. Take turns.

TELL A PROBLEM:	RESPOND:
My car isn't running. I'm not feeling well. My computer isn't working. My phone isn't working. My classes aren't going well. I can't go out tonight. Other: _____	Oh, that's too bad. I'm sorry to hear that.

⭐ GRAMMAR BRIEFING 1

Present Progressive Tense—Negative Statements

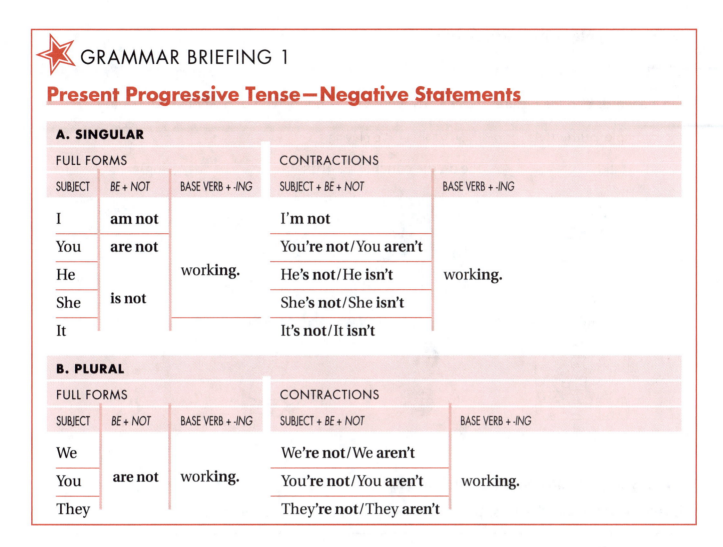

A. SINGULAR

FULL FORMS			CONTRACTIONS	
SUBJECT	BE + NOT	BASE VERB + -ING	SUBJECT + BE + NOT	BASE VERB + -ING
I	**am not**		I'm **not**	
You	**are not**		You're **not**/You **aren't**	
He		work**ing.**	He's **not**/He **isn't**	work**ing.**
She	**is not**		She's **not**/She **isn't**	
It			It's **not**/It **isn't**	

B. PLURAL

FULL FORMS			CONTRACTIONS	
SUBJECT	BE + NOT	BASE VERB + -ING	SUBJECT + BE + NOT	BASE VERB + -ING
We			We're **not**/We **aren't**	
You	**are not**	work**ing.**	You're **not**/You **aren't**	work**ing.**
They			They're **not**/They **aren't**	

1. Negative Statements with Contractions

Write negative statements in the present progressive. Use contractions. Change nouns (*Bob*) to pronouns (*he*).

	NOT	-N'T
1. Bob/sing	He's not singing.	He isn't singing.
2. I/reading		
3. the boys/play		
4. you/think		
5. it/rain		
6. Ms. Allen/talk		
7. we/sleep		

2. Making Negative Statements

Do the words and the pictures match? Say what's NOT happening and what IS happening.

Example   *Student A:* The radio isn't talking. It's playing.

1. (talk)   2. (lie on the couch) 3. (run)   4. (sing)

5. (driving the car) 6. (making coffee) 7. (wait for a bus) 8. (cry)

3. Negative Statements with Contractions

Use the words under the lines. Use the present progressive with contractions.

Dear Maja,

    I'm not going to classes today. __I'm not feeling__ well. _____ at
                                             1. I/not/feel   2. I/sit

my desk in my room. My roommate is here, too. _____ well either.
                                                       3. she/not/feel

She's in bed, but _____ . The TV is on, but _____ it.
                           4. she/not/sleep   5. we/not/watch

Outside, the sky is gray, and _____ . I can see some children with a
                                       6. the sun/not/shine

soccer ball, but _____ . _____ a little sad. I miss you!
                    7. they/not/play   8. I/feel

                                                      Love, Katya

GRAMMAR BRIEFING 2

Affirmative and Negative Statements with *Can*

Jan **can speak** Spanish.

Mack **can't understand** Jan.
He **can't speak** Spanish.

AFFIRMATIVE STATEMENTS		
SUBJECT	CAN	BASE VERB
I		
We		
You		
They	**can**	sing.
He		
She		
It		

NEGATIVE STATEMENTS		
SUBJECT	CAN + NOT	BASE VERB
I		
We		
You		
They	**cannot** **can't**	sing.
He		
She		
It		

 ## Talking the Talk

The /a/ in *can* is usually a very short sound.
  The /a/ in *can't* is a long sound.

WRITE	SAY
I can see it.	I /kn/ SEE it.
I can't see it.	I /KANT/ SEE it.

4. Pronunciation of *Can* vs. *Can't*

A. Listen and repeat.

1. I can drive.   I can't drive.

2. He can sing.   He can't sing.

3. I can cook.   I can't cook.

4. We can swim.   We can't swim.

5. He can speak English.   He can't speak English.

6. The baby can talk.   The baby can't talk.

B. Listen and circle the letter of the sentence you hear.

1. ⓐ She can sing.   b. She can't sing.   5. a. They can do it.   b. They can't do it.

2. a. He can sing.   b. He can't sing.   6. a. We can do it.   b. We can't do it.

3. a. I can drive.   b. I can't drive.   7. a. The baby can talk.   b. The baby can't talk.

4. a. She can drive.   b. She can't drive.   8. a. He can dance.   b. He can't dance.

C. Work with a partner. Take turns reading the answers to Part B.

5. Making Statements with *Can* and *Can't*

A. Student A: Say the things in the list that you can do. Student B: Listen and check (✓) those things. Say what Student A *cannot* do. Take turns.

Example *Student A:* I can speak English, I can drive a car, and I can make coffee.

   Student B: So, you can't speak Chinese, you can't . . . .

❏ speak English   ❏ drive a bus   ❏ run fast

❏ speak Chinese   ❏ dance   ❏ make coffee

❏ drive a car   ❏ sing   ❏ cook

B. Write things your partner can and cannot do.

1. _____ can _____   4. _____
   Your partner's name

2. He/She can _____   5. _____

3. _____   6. _____

⭐ GRAMMAR BRIEFING 3

Yes/No Questions with *Can*

YES/NO QUESTIONS				SHORT ANSWERS	
CAN	SUBJECT	BASE VERB		YES	NO
	you	**swim?**		Yes, I **can.**	No, I **can't.**
Can	Bob	**play**	baseball?	Yes, he **can.**	No, he **can't.**
	they	**fix**	your car?	Yes, they **can.**	No, they **can't.**

---

6. Yes/No Questions and Short Answers with *Can*

A. Complete the conversations.

1. *A:* <u>Can you</u> _____ speak French?   3. *A:* _____ you _____ Spanish?

   B: _____ , I can't.   *B:* Yes, _____ speak it a little.

2. *A:* _____ your father cook?   4. *A:* _____ with your left hand?

   B: Yes, _____ . He cooks   *B:* No, _____ . I'm right-handed.

   dinner every night.   I can only write with my right hand.

B. Work alone or with a partner. Write two conversations. Use *yes/no* questions with *Can*.

1. *A:* _____

   B: _____

2. *A:* _____

   B: _____

7. Asking and Answering Questions with *Can*

A. Walk around the room. Ask your classmates questions with *Can you. . . ?* Write a name in each box. Answer your classmates' questions with *Yes, I can.* or *No, I can't.*

Example *Student A:* Maria, can you swim?

   Student B: Yes, I can.   (Student A writes *Maria* in the box.)

	CAN	CAN'T		CAN	CAN'T
swim			ride a bicycle		
play the guitar			ride a horse		
fix a car			use a computer		

B. Talk about your classmates. What can they do? What can't they do?

C. Write about your classmates. Write ten statements with *can* and *can't* on a piece of paper.

Example Maria can swim.

GRAMMAR BRIEFING 4

And, But, and Or

A. USING CONJUNCTIONS

1. *And, but,* and *or* are **conjunctions.**
   They can connect:

   • Words.

   • Groups of words.

   • Sentences.

   > Oscar **and** Susan are married.
   >
   > They're at home **or** in school.
   >
   > Miho is in class, **but** Oscar is absent.

2. *And* adds information.

   > Katya **and** Miho are friends.
   >   (Katya + Miho)

3. *But* shows that something is surprising or different.

   > That runner is old **but** fast!
   >
   > This photo is bad, **but** that photo is good.

4. *Or* shows a choice between things.

   > He can write with his left hand **or** his right hand.

B. COMMAS BEFORE CONJUNCTIONS

1. Use a **comma** (,) before *and/but/or* when they connect sentences.

   > sentence   +   sentence

2. Do not use a comma before *and/but/or* when they connect words.

   > word + word
   >
   > Ellen can <u>sing</u> and <u>dance</u>.
   >   /

8. Connecting Words *vs.* Connecting Sentences

Look at *and, but,* and *or* in these sentences. Do they connect <u>words</u> or <u>sentences</u>? Write *w* or *s.*

1. Hassan is tall, but his brother isn't. _s_

2. Is Susan or Oscar at home? ____

3. His car is red, and her car is blue. ____

4. I can't dance or sing. ____

5. I have my pen, but where is your pen? ____

6. He can speak English and French. ____

7. Is he a fast runner, or is he slow? ____

8. The house is small but expensive. ____

9. She has one brother and one sister. ____

10. Can you fix it, or can he do it? ____

9. Listen for Conjunctions

Listen to the conversation. Write the word you hear: *and, but,* or *or.*

Miho: Oscar, Katya __and__ I are having a party. Can you _____ Susan come?
          ₁   ₂

Oscar: Sounds great! When?

Miho: I think on Friday night _____ maybe on Saturday. We're not sure.
                              ₃

Oscar: Friday's good, _____ Saturday isn't. We have a baby-sitter on Friday _____
                       ₄   ₅

        not on Saturday.

Miho: That's OK—bring the baby!

Oscar: What else can we bring?

Miho: Oh, something to eat _____ drink. We'll have pizza _____ soda _____
                             ₆   ₇   ₈

        chips _____ popcorn—things like that.
              ₉

Oscar: Sounds good. What time?

Miho: I'll call you later!

Oscar: OK.

a baby-sitter = a person who watches a child when the mother and father aren't home.

10. Using *And* and *But*

A. Form a group of three. Think about your two partners. What's the same about both of them? On a piece of paper, write two sentences with *and*. What's different? Write two sentences with *but*.

Examples Le and Tran are Vietnamese.

          Le has a car, but Tran can't drive.

B. Share your sentences. Is the information correct?

EXTRA PRACTICE

11. Negative Statements in the Present Progressive

Write negative statements in the present progressive. Use contractions.

1. (he/sleep) _He's not sleeping._ OR _He isn't sleeping._ _____

2. (I/feel/well today) _____

3. (Bob and Mary/dance) _____

4. (this computer/work) _____

5. (the people in the picture/smile) _____

6. (you/help) _____

7. (the sun/shine) _____

8. (it/rain) _____

12. Statements with *Can*

A. Write five statements about things you can do. Write them on a piece of paper.

Example   I can play the piano.

B. Write statements with the words in parentheses. Use the two forms of *can* + *not*.

1. Young-Eun is eight years old.   a. _____

   (she/drive a car)   b. _____

2. Please speak a little louder.   a. _____

   (we/hear you)   b. _____

3. Khalil is sick.   a. _____

   (he/go to school)   b. _____

13. *Yes/No* Questions and Answers with *Can*

Complete the conversations. Use *can't* in short answers with *No.*

1. *A:* _____ drive a car?

   B: _____ , I can.

2. *A:* _____ Ms. Allen

   _____ Russian?

   B: No, _____ , but she

   can speak Arabic.

3. *A:* _____ write with your left hand?

   B: No, _____ . I'm right-handed.

4. *A:* _____ your friends _____ ?

   B: Yes, _____ . They sing well.

5. *A:* _____ ?

   B: No, _____ . I can't sing at all!

14. Conjunctions *And, But,* and *Or*

A. Match the first and last part of each sentence.

_____ 1. Jack and Liz can't sing,

_____ 2. Siok and Han can't sing

_____ 3. Tomoko can sing,

_____ 4. Carmen can sing in English

a. or dance.

b. or in Spanish.

c. but they can dance.

d. and she can dance, too.

B. Write *and, but,* or *or.*

1. Baseball _____ tennis are sports.

2. Is he married _____ single?

3. I have a brother _____ a sister.

4. I speak English _____ not French.

5. His name is Bob _____ Bill.

6. I can dance _____ not sing.

C. Write six sentences with conjunctions. Use *and, but,* and *or.*

Example Do you have sisters or brothers?

Unit 3 Wrap-Up Activities

1. A Class Party: READING

Read this paragraph.

It's Friday afternoon. Miho and Katya are at a party in a classroom. They're standing by the windows. Thirty students are in the room. There's music, and people are talking. There are drinks and pizza on the teacher's desk. Miho is speaking Japanese with a friend. Katya isn't listening. She can't speak Japanese, and she can't understand their conversation. She's thinking about a new student in her class. He's standing by the blackboard, and he's smiling at her. He has nice eyes and a great smile.

2. A Party on Saturday Night: WRITING

It's Saturday evening. You are at a party. Who is there? What are they doing? Write about the party. Use verbs in the present progressive.

3. A Party for My Grandmother: EDITING

Correct the 8 errors. The first one is corrected for you.

It's Sunday afternoon at my grandmother's
                    and
house, but we're having a party. About 30 friend and relatives are here. Good music playing. Everybody can to dance to this music. My brothers dancing with their wifes. I'm can see my grandmother. She is haveing a good time. It's her birthday.

4. Ask Your Classmates: SPEAKING/LISTENING

A. Work with a partner. Practice making questions with *Can you* and *Are you* from statements 1–8.

B. Walk around the room. Ask your classmates the questions. Write different names on the lines. Make true statements.

Example   *Student A:*   Cheeyung, can you read music?

                 Student B: Yes, I can.

                 Student A writes: ___Cheeyung___ can read music.

1. _____ can read music.

2. _____ is left-handed.

3. _____ is wearing a necklace.

4. _____ can speak Spanish.

5. _____ is hungry.

6. _____ is feeling sleepy.

7. _____ can cook.

8. _____ is planning a trip.

5. An Invitation to a Party: SPEAKING/LISTENING

Work with a partner. It's Saturday night. You are talking on the phone. Complete and act out this conversation:

Student A: Hello, _____ ! This is _____ .

Student B: Hi, _____ ! How are you?

Student A: I'm fine, thanks. I'm calling because we're having a party. Can you come?

Student B: When? Where?

Student A: Right now! At _____ .

Student A: Who's there? What are you doing?

Student B: . . . .

Ways to end the conversation:

Student A: I'm sorry, but I can't come.

Student B: That's too bad! OK, see you later.

Student A: Bye!

Student A: I can come right away.

Student B: Great! See you soon!

Student A: Bye!

GRAMMAR SUMMARY

Present Progressive Tense

AFFIRMATIVE STATEMENTS

FULL FORM	CONTRACTIONS
I **am** going.	I**'m** going.
We/You/They **are** going.	We/You/They**'re** going.
He/She/It **is** going.	He/She/It**'s** going.

NEGATIVE STATEMENTS

FULL FORM	CONTRACTIONS	
I **am not** moving.	I**'m not**	
	We/You/They**'re not**	
We/You/They **are not** moving.	We/You/They **aren't**	**moving.**
	He/She/It**'s not**	
He/She/It **is not** moving.	He/She/It **isn't**	

YES/NO QUESTIONS AND SHORT ANSWERS

QUESTIONS	SHORT ANSWERS	
Am I do**ing** the right exercise?	Yes, I **am.**	No, I**'m not.**
Is he/she/it do**ing** a good job?	Yes, he/she/it **is.**	No, he/she/it**'s not.**
		No, he/she/it **isn't.**
Are we/you/they do**ing** well?	Yes, we/you/they **are.**	No, we/you/they**'re not.**
		No, we/you/they **aren't.**

QUESTIONS WITH *WHAT*

QUESTIONS	ANSWERS
What are you do**ing**?	I'm studying.
What are you study**ing**?	English.

★ See the Grammar Briefings on pages 78, 81, 83, and 95.

Can

AFFIRMATIVE AND NEGATIVE STATEMENTS

AFFIRMATIVE	NEGATIVE
I / We/You/They / He/She/It **can** do it.	I / We/You/They / He/She/It **cannot** / **can't** do it.

YES/NO QUESTIONS AND SHORT ANSWERS

QUESTIONS	SHORT ANSWERS	
Can I/we/you/they/he/she/it **do** it?	Yes, I/we/you/they/he/she/it **can.**	No, I/we/you/they/he/she/it **can't.**

★ See the Grammar Briefings on pages 97 and 99.

Plural Nouns

SINGULAR	PLURAL
student	students
class	classes
potato	potatoes
knife	knives

★ See the Grammar Briefing on page 88.

Conjunctions *And*, *But*, and *Or*

and	Bob **and** Mary can sing.
but	Bob can sing, **but** Mary can't.
or	The class is in Room 116 **or** 126. I can't remember.

★ See the Grammar Briefing on page 100.

TEST YOURSELF ON CHAPTER 5

1. Write affirmative statements in the present progressive. Use full forms.

   1. (we/go to a party) _We are going to a party_.

   2. (the man/carry a briefcase) _____

   3. (you/make a mistake) _____

   4. (the movie/begin) _____

   5. (the children/get hungry) _____

2. Write *yes/no* questions and short answers.

   1. you/listen (yes) _Are you listening?   Yes, I am._

   2. he/use the phone (yes) _____

   3. the boys/wait (no) _____

3. Put the words in order. Write the questions. Match them with their answers.

   1. are / what / they / doing   _What are they doing?_   _____ a. Jeans and a T-shirt.

   2. she / doing / is / what   _____   _1_ b. Making a movie.

   3. you / wearing / are / what   _____   _____ c. A cup of coffee.

   4. watching / what / they / are   _____   _____ d. A basketball game.

   5. is / holding / what / he   _____   _____ e. Fixing her car.

4. Write the plural forms of these nouns.

   1. sister   _sisters_____   6. fax   _____

   2. class   _____   7. tooth   _____

   3. party   _____   8. leaf   _____

   4. knife   _____   9. baby   _____

   5. eye   _____   10. radio   _____

5. Find the six errors and correct them.

   1. My feet ~~is~~ *are* cold.   4. We're do homework right now.

   2. The game starting now.   5. My sunglasses is new.

   3. Your friend is he having a good time?   6. What you are cooking?

109

TEST YOURSELF ON CHAPTER 6

6. Make the sentences negative. Use contractions.

1. The sun is shining now. _The sun isn't shining now._
2. My sister and I are planning a party. _____
3. His wife is having a baby. _____
4. I am thinking about school. _____
5. You are listening to me. _____

7. Write sentences with *can* or *can't*. Use the information in the chart.

CAN THEY . . .	SUSAN	OSCAR	
speak Italian?	YES	NO	1. _Susan can speak Italian._
			2. _____
fix a car?	NO	YES	3. _____
			4. _____

8. Write *yes/no* questions with *can*. Write the short answers.

1. Hank/play the piano (yes) _Can Hank play the piano? Yes, he can._
2. that man/ read music (no) _____
3. you/go to school by bus (yes) _____
4. Luisa/ride a horse (no) _____

9. Write *and*, *but*, or *or*.

1. Susan _and_ Oscar are married.
2. Is your car new _____ old?
3. My brother can sing, _____ I can't.
4. I'm in class, _____ I'm listening.
5. She is tall, _____ her sister isn't.
6. Is he married _____ single?

10. Find the six errors and correct them.

1. My brother ~~he's~~ *is* not working.
2. His girlfriend can to speak Spanish.
3. They're aren't shopping.
4. We're having pizza, and soda.
5. Can they fix it? No, they're can't.
6. It isn't rain today.

See Answer Key pages ANS-3 and ANS-4.

Everyday Life

Chapter 7

Daily Routines

- Simple present tense:
  Affirmative statements
  Yes/No questions and short answers
  Spelling rules
- Present progressive vs. simple present

Chapter 8

Would You Like Something?

- Simple present tense:
  Negative statements
  Wh- questions
- Adverbs of frequency
- *I'd like . . .* and *Would you like . . . ?*

CHAPTER 7
Daily Routines

GRAMMAR IN ACTION

Reading and Listening

A. Listen and read.

> *Narrator:* It's 8:30 on Tuesday morning. Angie is waiting for the bus. She's going to school.
>
> *Angie:* Hi, Martin! What are you doing on the bus? You always drive to school.
>
> *Martin:* Yes, but today, my brother's using my car. He sometimes borrows it.
>
> *Angie:* I see.
>
> *Martin:* Do you take the bus every day?
>
> *Angie:* No, not every day, just on Tuesdays and Thursdays.
>
> *Martin:* What about the other days? Do you have a car?
>
> *Angie:* Yes, we do, but my husband needs it for his job. I usually get a ride from a friend, sometimes from Zulma.
>
> *Martin:* She drives an old blue Chevy, right?
>
> *Angie:* Yeah, it's *REALLY* old, but it runs!

borrow = take something to use and then give back (*borrow money from a bank, borrow a pen from a classmate*)

B. Work with a partner. Practice the conversation in Part A.

Think about Grammar

A. Complete the sentences from the conversation.

1. What _are you doing_____ on the bus?

2. You _____ drive to school.

3. Yes, but _____ , my brother's using my car.

4. He _____ borrows it.

5. Do you take the bus _____ ?

6. No, not every day, just _____ .

7. _____ the other days?

8. I _____ get a ride from a friend, sometimes from Zulma.

B. Circle the simple present verb from the conversation. <u>Underline</u> the subject of the verb. Then complete the rule.

1. <u>You</u> always (drive/drives) to school.

2. He sometimes (borrow/borrows) it.

3. I (see/sees).

4. I usually (get/gets) a ride from a friend.

5. She (drive/drives) an old blue Chevy.

6. It's really old, but it (run/runs)!

RULE: Simple present verbs end in –*s* after the subject pronouns _he___ , _____ ,

and _____ .

C. Circle your answers. Ask your partner. Circle your partner's answers.

	YOU		YOUR PARTNER	
1. Do you take the bus sometimes?	Yes, I do.	No, I don't.	Yes, I do.	No, I don't.
2. Do you have a car?	Yes, I do.	No, I don't.	Yes, I do.	No, I don't.
3. Do you get rides from friends?	Yes, I do.	No, I don't.	Yes, I do.	No, I don't.
4. How do you get to school?	by bus	on foot	by bus	on foot
	by car	_____	by car	_____

GRAMMAR BRIEFING 1

Simple Present Tense—Affirmative Statements

SUBJECT	BASE VERB		SUBJECT	BASE VERB + -S	
I			He		
We			She		
You	**work**	every day.	It	**works**	every day.
They			My friend Lili		
My friends					

 ## Grammar Hotspot!

In the simple present tense, **third person singular** verbs end in *-s*. These are the verbs after:

- Singular nouns (for example, *a boy, Mrs. Brown, her book*).

> **Jack** loves his car.
>
> **His car** looks new.

- Third person singular subject pronouns (*he, she,* and *it*).

> **He** drives a Toyota.

1. Third Person Singular Subjects

Check (✓) the sentences with third person singular subjects.

_____ 1. I love music.

✓ 2. My brother lives in Texas.

_____ 3. Laura talks fast.

_____ 4. You do good work.

_____ 5. It's cold.

_____ 6. Mr. and Mrs. West aren't here.

_____ 7. She is a good friend.

_____ 8. Children need lots of sleep.

_____ 9. People in Japan speak Japanese.

_____ 10. The door is open.

2. Verb Forms in Simple Present Tense Statements

Complete the statements. Use the simple present tense of the verb in parentheses ( ).

1. (drive)

a. Viktor __drives__ a nice car.

b. Carl and Nancy _____ to work.

c. We _____ to school.

2. (take)

a. Al and I _____ the bus to school.

b. He _____ the bus every day.

c. You _____ a taxi sometimes.

3. (work)

a. She _____ every day.

b. I _____ after school.

c. This camera _____ underwater.

4. (eat)

a. Jan _____ at 7:00 p.m.

b. The cat _____ in the kitchen.

c. They _____ pizza on Fridays.

3. Simple Present Tense Statements with *He* and *She*

A. Talk about these people's jobs. Ask *What does* (name) *do?* Use the words in the box.

Example   *Student A:* What does Tom do?
          Student B: He makes bagels.

| drive a bus | make furniture | sell cars | give advice |
| drive a truck | make bagels | sell make-up | give the news |

1. Tom   2. Jennifer   3. Miguel   4. Elsa

5. Ed   6. Lisa   7. Nancy   8. Tony

B. Look at the people in Part A. Who do you think has a good job? Who has a bad job? Why?

GRAMMAR BRIEFING 2

Simple Present Tense Verbs after Third Person Singular Subjects

A. AFFIRMATIVE STATEMENTS

THIRD PERSON SINGULAR SUBJECT	BASE VERB + -(E)S	
He	**plays**	basketball.
She	**writes**	stories.
It	**opens**	at 9:00 a.m.
Maria	**watches**	movies every night.
The bus	**carries**	children to school.

B. SPELLING RULES

Add -*s* or -*es* to the base verb after third person singular subjects:

- Most verbs:
  Add -*s*.

  eat ➜ eat**s**
  wake up ➜ wake**s** up

- Verbs ending in *ch, s, sh, x,* or *z*:
  Add -*es*.

  kiss ➜ kiss**es**
  brush ➜ brush**es**
  fix ➜ fix**es**

- Verbs ending in a consonant + *y*:
  Change *y* to *i* and add -*es*.

  study ➜ stud**ies**
  carry ➜ carr**ies**

 Grammar Hotspot!

In the simple present tense, the verbs *have, go,* and *do* are **irregular** after third person singular subjects.

I **have**/She **has** a full-time job.

I **go**/He **goes** to work by car.

I **do**/She **does** the homework at the library.

4. Spelling of Third Person Singular Verbs

A. Complete the statements. Use the verb in parentheses.

1. (cook) She _cooks_ dinner at 6:00.
2. (enjoy) He _____ good food.
3. (do) He _____ all his homework.
4. (want) Bob _____ a new car.
5. (go) Ann _____ shopping every weekend.

6. (watch) She _____ TV at night.
7. (miss) He _____ his girlfriend.
8. (cry) The baby _____ sometimes.
9. (play) She _____ many sports.
10. (wake up) My daughter _____ at 7:00 every morning.

B. Complete the sentences. Use the verbs in the box. Use the simple present tense.

ask	carry	have	match	start	teach	wash	wear

1. Mark _____ nice clothes.
2. Jill _____ all the dishes.
3. Dr. Lind _____ math.
4. Your tie _____ your shirt.

5. Lou _____ a part-time job.
6. That girl _____ many questions.
7. Bill _____ a briefcase to work.
8. The class _____ at 9:00.

5. Verb Forms in Simple Present Tense Statements

Write the simple present tense. Use the verbs in parentheses ( ).

Mehmet is a student. He _studies_ 1 (study) at the University of California. He

_____ 2 (have) an apartment near the university. He _____ 3 (share) the apartment

with two other students. Every day, Mehmet _____ 4 (go) to classes.

Mehmet _____ 5 (come) from Turkey. His mother and father _____ 6 (live) in

Istanbul. His mother _____ 7 (call) him every Sunday. She _____ 8 (worry) about

her son. Mehmet always _____ 9 (say), "Don't worry! I'm OK!" He _____ 10 (miss)

his family and friends back home. He _____ 11 (write) many e-mail messages to his

friends, and they _____ 12 (write) to him. He _____ 13 (like) getting mail.

Talking the Talk

Sometimes the *-(e)s* at the end of a verb adds a syllable.

ONE SYLLABLE	TWO SYLLABLES
•	• •
use	uses
kiss	kisses
fix	fixes
I watch TV.	He watches TV.

6. Pronunciation of Verbs

A. Does the *-(e)s* add a syllable? Circle your answers.

       •   •

1. I **live** on Green Street. She **lives** on Green St.   Yes   (No)

       •   • •

2. They **teach** English. He **teaches** English.   (Yes)   No

3. We **miss** our friends. He **misses** his friends.   Yes   No

4. You **listen** in class. She **listens** in class.   Yes   No

5. We **eat** fruit. It **eats** fruit.   Yes   No

6. They **fix** cars. He **fixes** cars.   Yes   No

7. You **study** math. She **studies** math.   Yes   No

8. They **finish** at 10:00. It **finishes** at 10:00.   Yes   No

9. I **play** basketball. He **plays** basketball.   Yes   No

10. We **use** computers. She **uses** computers.   Yes   No

B. Listen to the statements. Check your answers to Part A.

C. Work with a partner. Say the statements in Part A. Take turns.

7. Using Simple Present Tense Verbs

A. Read about Rita's morning routine.

Rita says, "I wake up at 6:30 every day. I get up, and I go to the bathroom. I take a shower, and I get dressed. I have breakfast, and I listen to the radio in the kitchen. After breakfast, I brush my teeth. Then I put on my make-up, and I fix my hair. I put on my coat, and I leave my apartment at 7:45."

B. Work with a partner. Look at the pictures. Take turns saying what Rita does every morning.

Example *Student A:* She wakes up at 6:30.

C. Write about Rita's morning routine.

8. Using Simple Present Tense Verbs

A. How do you begin your day? Take turns talking about your morning routine. Listen and take notes about the other people in the group.

> *Notes*
> *Meng – wakes up @ 7:00,*
> *shower, kitchen, radio, . . .*

B. Write about the morning routine of a person in your group. Use simple present tense verbs.

Example   Meng wakes up at seven o'clock. First, he takes a shower
and gets dressed. Then he goes into the kitchen. . .

9. Using Simple Present Tense Verbs

Work with a partner. Choose a person from photo 1, 2, or 3. Invent information about the person. Tell your partner about him or her.

Example   This is Michael. He is a doctor. He lives in New York. He isn't married. He has a girlfriend. He works in a hospital. He likes his job. He likes music. He drives a nice car.

1.

2.

3.

⭐ GRAMMAR BRIEFING 3

Simple Present *Yes/No* Questions and Short Answers

YES/NO QUESTIONS			
DO/DOES	SUBJECT	BASE VERB	
Do	I we you they	**need**	a car?
Does	he she it	**work**	every day?

SHORT ANSWERS					
YES			NO		
Yes,	I we you they	**do.**	No,	I we you they	**don't.**
	he she it	**does.**		he she it	**doesn't.**

☀ **Grammar Hotspot!**

Remember! *Yes/No* questions with the verb *be* do not use *do/does.*

QUESTIONS WITH *BE*	QUESTIONS WITH OTHER VERBS
Are you ready?	**Do you need** more time?
Is he a good student?	**Does he do** much homework?
Are they at home now?	**Do they live** in an apartment?

10. *Do* vs. *Does, Don't* vs. *Doesn't*

Write *do* or *does, don't* or *doesn't.*

1. *A:* __Does__ John live in New York?

    B: Yes, he _____ .

2. *A:* _____ you like pizza?

    B: Yes, I _____ .

3. *A:* _____ she like her job?

    B: No, she _____ .

4. *A:* _____ we have time for coffee?

    B: Yes, we _____ .

5. *A:* _____ George speak Spanish?

    B: No, he _____ .

6. *A:* _____ you play the piano or the guitar?

    B: No, I _____ .

11. *Yes/No Questions and Short Answers*

A. Complete the *yes/no* questions with the verbs in parentheses ( ). Complete the short answers.

Mrs. Smith: (work) <u>Do</u> you and your sister <u>work</u> at McDonalds?

　　　　　　　　　　　 1　　　　　　　　　　　　　　 2

Julie:　　　　Yes, <u>we do</u> . We both work there part-time.
　　　　　　　　　　 3

Mrs. Smith: (make) What do you do, Julie? _____ you _____ hamburgers?
　　　　　　　　　　　　　　　　　　　　　　 4　　　　　 5

Julie:　　　　No, _____ . I work at the cash register.
　　　　　　　　　 6

Mrs. Smith: (take) I see. So, _____ you _____ orders for food?
　　　　　　　　　　　　　 7　　　　　 8

Julie:　　　　Yes, _____ . I take the orders, and people pay me.
　　　　　　　　　 9

Mrs. Smith: (work) What about your sister? _____ she _____ at the register, too?
　　　　　　　　　　　　　　　　　　　　 10　　　　　　 11

Julie:　　　　Yes, _____ . Kate sometimes works in the kitchen, too.
　　　　　　　　　 12

Mrs. Smith: (like) _____ you _____ working at McDonalds?
　　　　　　　　　 13　　　　　 14

Julie:　　　　Yes, _____ . I see lots of my friends there, and I like the food.
　　　　　　　　　 15

Mrs. Smith: (like) What about Kate? _____ she _____ working there?
　　　　　　　　　　　　　　　　 16　　　　　 17

Julie:　　　　No, _____ . She's getting tired of hamburgers and french fries!
　　　　　　　　 18

B. Listen to the conversation. Check your answers to Part A.

💬 Talking the Talk

There are many ways to answer "Yes" or "No."

QUESTION	FORMAL CONVERSATION		INFORMAL CONVERSATION	
	YES	NO	YES	NO
			Uh-huh.	Uh-uh.
Do you work full-time?	Yes, I do.	No, I don't.	Yup.	Nope.
			Yeah.	Nah.

12. Informal Ways to Answer *Yes* and *No*

Listen to the informal conversations. You will hear each conversation twice (two times). Does the speaker answer *Yes* or *No?* Circle your answers.

Conversation 1:   (Yes)   No   Conversation 4:   Yes   No

Conversation 2:   Yes   No   Conversation 5:   Yes   No

Conversation 3:   Yes   No   Conversation 6:   Yes   No

13. Asking *Do You* Questions and Giving Short Answers

A. Work with a partner. Look at statements 1–6 in Part B. Change them to questions with *Do you . . . ?* Practice the questions.

B. Walk around in your classroom. Ask your classmates the questions. Answer questions with *Yes, I do.* or *No, I don't.* Write different names on the lines. Make true statements.

Example   *Student A:* Yuri, do you like hamburgers?

Student B: No, I don't.

Student A: Nelson, do you like hamburgers?

Student C: Yes, I do.

Student A can write: ___Nelson___ likes hamburgers.

1. _____ likes hamburgers.

2. _____ eats hamburgers with ketchup.

3. _____ goes to McDonalds sometimes.

4. _____ drinks tea.

5. _____ likes pizza.

6. _____ feels hungry now.

GRAMMAR BRIEFING 4

Present Progressive vs. Simple Present

A. PRESENT PROGRESSIVE

1. Use present progressive for actions happening now.

> You **are reading** these words.
>
> We **are studying** English.

2. Here are examples of **time expressions** with present progressive verbs.

> Shh! The baby's sleeping **right now.**
>
> He is going to Boston College **this year.**
>
> **These days,** many people are looking for jobs.

B. SIMPLE PRESENT

1. Use simple present for:

   • Habits.

> I **drink** coffee for breakfast.

   • Repeated actions.

> The store **closes** at 9:30 p.m.

   • Things that are always true.

> Fish **swim** in the sea.

2. Here are examples of time expressions with simple present verbs.

> He reads the newspaper **every day.**
>
> **On weekends,** they go to movies.
>
> She calls her family **once a week.**

 Grammar Hotspot!

1. Use *am, is, are* with *-ing* verbs. Do not use *am, is, are* + base verb.

> He is living with a friend.
>   **NOT:** He ~~is live~~ with a friend.

2. Use the simple present, not the present progressive, for the verbs *want, need, know,* and *like*. These are **non-action** (or **stative**) **verbs.**

> She knows my phone number.
>   **NOT:** She~~'s knowing~~ my phone number.
>
> I need a computer now.
>   **NOT:** I~~'m needing~~ a computer now.

14. Recognizing Present Progressive and Simple Present

<u>Underline</u> the verbs in the sentences. There are eight simple present verbs and seven present progressive verbs. Write *simple* or *prog.* The first two verbs are done for you.

               simple   *prog.*

Hye-Jung <u>comes</u> from Korea. She<u>'s studying</u> English in the United States. At this

moment, she's talking on the phone with her mother. They're speaking Korean.

Hye-Jung calls home once a week. She always speaks Korean with her family.

    Hye-Jung is living with her friend Tomoko. They have an apartment. Tomoko comes

from Japan, so she speaks Japanese. She knows English, too. Hye-Jung and Tomoko

speak English together. Right now, Tomoko is sitting at her desk in her bedroom. She's

drinking tea, and she's studying.

15. Present Progressive vs. Simple Present

Circle the correct verb.

1. I (want/am wanting) new shoes.
2. This bus is (go/going) downtown.
3. Henry (likes/is liking) horror movies.
4. Right now, he (talks/is talking) on the phone.
5. She's (take/taking) driving lessons.
6. The students (know/are knowing) the answers.
7. Every day, Nancy (reads/is reading) her e-mail.
8. Nick (wants/is wanting) pizza for lunch.
9. I (need/am needing) an eraser.
10. I'm (study/studying) English.
11. The teacher (knows/is knowing) all the names.
12. The cat is (sleeps/sleeping).
13. They (eat/are eating) in a restaurant once a week
14. Ann (visits/is visiting) her sister in Miami this week.

16. Using Present Progressive and Simple Present

A. Look at the people in the pictures. What do they do *every day?* What are they doing *right now?* Take turns telling about them. Use the words in the box and your own words.

Example   *Student A:* This woman is a teacher.

Student B: Every day, she teaches little children.

Student C: Right now, she is . . . .

go to court	help customers	talk in court	throw the ball
read	play baseball	teach little children	show things on sale

1. A teacher

2. A baseball player

3. A salesperson

4. A lawyer

B. Choose a picture from Part A. On a piece of paper, write four statements about the person. Use the simple present tense and the present progressive.

Example   The man in the picture is a baseball player.

1. Every day, he goes to the baseball park.

2. Right now, he is. . . .

EXTRA PRACTICE

17. Verb Forms in Simple Present Tense Statements

Write the simple present tense. Use the verbs in parentheses ( ).

Rosalie is a student. She _____ classes at Brixton Community College.
  1 (take)

Her classes _____ Monday to Friday. On weekends, she _____ .
  2 (meet)   3 (work)

Her mother and father _____ a small restaurant, and Rosalie _____
  4 (own)   5 (help)

at the restaurant. Her brothers and sisters _____ there, too. The restaurant
  6 (work)

_____ great Mexican food. Rosalie _____ , "The restaurant is
  7 (serve)   8 (say)

always busy, so we always _____ hard!"
  9 (work)

18. Simple Present Tense Affirmative Statements

Choose a person from the photos on page 120. Write five statements about the person. Use five different simple present tense verbs.

Example *The man in the photo lives in London. He . . . .*

19. *Yes/No Questions in the Simple Present*

A. Circle the correct form of the verb.

1. Do you (speak/speaking) English?
2. Does he (has/have) a job?
3. (Do/Does) she work on weekends?
4. (Are/Do) you like your job?
5. Does this bus (go/goes) to Main St.?
6. Do they (take/taking) the bus to work?
7. (Are/Do) you sometimes take the bus?
8. (Is/Does) Yoshi have a car?
9. (Are/Do) they work together?
10. (Is/Does) he do a good job?
11. Does it (rain/rains) much here?
12. (Do/Does) Mr. and Mrs. Shu live there?
13. (Are/Do) you have a watch?
14. Does she (do/does) much homework?

B. Write three questions with *Do you* to ask your classmates.

1. _____

2. _____

3. _____

20. Present Progressive vs. Simple Present

A. Circle the correct verb.

1. He (is wanting/wants) a new job.

2. I'm (work/working) today.

3. You (know/are knowing) my number.

4. They (need/are needing) money.

5. She's (speak/speaking) Japanese.

6. I (like/am liking) this picture.

B. Complete the statements. Use the verb in parentheses in the simple present AND the present progressive.

1. (make) Miguel _____ furniture.

a

   Right now, he _____ something in his workshop.

b

2. (work) Jennifer _____ right now.

a

   She _____ for Channel 7 News in Dallas.

b

3. (bake) Tom is in the kitchen. He _____ some bagels.

a

   Every week, he _____ hundreds of bagels.

b

4. (talk) Lisa _____ to people about make-up.

a

   She _____ to a customer at the moment.

b

CHAPTER 8

Would You Like Something?

GRAMMAR IN ACTION

Reading and Listening

A. Listen and read.

Narrator: Angie, Martin, and Zulma are at school. It's almost time for class, but they have ten minutes. They're in the cafeteria.

Angie: I need more coffee! Martin, would you like some more?

Martin: No, thanks. I'm fine.

Angie: Zulma, what about you? Would you like something to drink?

Zulma: What do they have? I don't usually drink coffee.

Angie: They have orange juice, there's tea, . . .

Zulma: Oh, I'd like some tea. Thanks.

Angie: No problem.

Martin: My wife never drinks coffee. It always gives her headaches.

Zulma: It doesn't give me headaches, but I don't like the taste!

B. Form a group of three. Practice the conversation in Part A.

Think about Grammar

A. Complete these sentences from Reading and Listening, Part A.

1. *Angie:* I need more coffee! Martin, <u>would you like</u> some more?

2. *Martin:* _____ . I'm fine.

3. *Angie:* Zulma, what about you? _____ something to drink?

4. *Zulma:* What _____ ? I _____ coffee.

5. *Zulma:* Oh, _____ some tea. Thanks.

6. *Angie:* No _____ .

7. *Martin:* My wife _____ drinks coffee. It _____ gives her headaches.

8. *Zulma:* It _____ me headaches, but I _____ the taste!

B. Read the statements in the chart below. Circle your choices.

C. Ask questions with *Do you*. Circle the choices for your partner.

Example   *Student A:* Do you usually drink coffee in the morning?
             Student B: No, I don't. I drink tea.
             Student A circles "doesn't usually drink."

YOU	YOUR PARTNER
1. I (usually drink/don't usually drink) coffee in the morning.	1. My partner (usually drinks/doesn't usually drink) coffee in the morning.
2. I (eat/don't eat) breakfast every morning.	2. My partner (eats/doesn't eat) breakfast every morning.
3. I usually (buy/make) my lunch.	3. My partner usually (buys/makes) lunch.
4. I (have/don't have) my lunch at school.	4. My partner (has/doesn't have) lunch at school.
5. I (usually eat/don't usually eat) dinner with my family.	5. My partner (usually eats/doesn't usually eat) with (his/her) family.

GRAMMAR BRIEFING 1

Simple Present Tense—Negative Statements

FULL FORMS					CONTRACTIONS			
SUBJECT	DO/DOES	NOT	BASE VERB		SUBJECT	DON'T/DOESN'T	BASE VERB	
I					I			
We	**do**				We	**don't**		
You		**not**	**drink**	milk.	You		**drink**	milk.
They					They			
He					He			
She	**does**				She	**doesn't**		
It					It			

Grammar Hotspot!

1. Use only the base verb after *does not/doesn't*. Do not add *-(e)s*.

   She does not have breakfast.
   NOT: She does not ~~has~~ breakfast.

2. Do not use forms of *be* to make present tense verbs negative.

   Jack doesn't live here.
   NOT: Jack ~~isn't~~ live here.

1. Negative Statements, Full Forms and Contractions

A. Write negative statements. Use full forms.

1. I/have/much free time

   I do not have much free time.

2. we/use/computers in class

   _____

3. our teacher/speak/Russian

   _____

4. the sun/shine/at night

   _____

5. cats/eat/fruit

   _____

6. you/need/glasses

   _____

B. Underline the full forms of *do/does not* in Part A. Write contractions.

Example   I <u>do not</u> have much free time.   *don't*

2. Making Negative Statements

A. Read the statements about Angie and Phil. Listen to the story. Are the statements true or false? Check (✓) your answers.

1. Angie and Phil live in a big house.   ❏ True   ❏ False

2. They have a big kitchen.   ❏ True   ❏ False

3. Phil likes to cook.   ❏ True   ❏ False

4. Angie enjoys good food.   ❏ True   ❏ False

5. She washes the dishes.   ❏ True   ❏ False

6. They go to nice restaurants.   ❏ True   ❏ False

B. Correct the false statements in Part A. Make them negative.

                  don't live

Example   1. Angie and Phil ~~live~~ in a big house.

3. Affirmative and Negative Statements

A. Work with a partner. Look at the foods in the pictures. What do you like? What do you eat every day? Take turns making affirmative and negative statements about all the foods.

Example   *Student A:* I like apples and oranges.

                 Student B: I like oranges, but I don't eat apples.

apples, oranges, bananas   *fried eggs, toast, and bacon*   *cake*   *ice cream*

broccoli and carrots   *rice*   *spaghetti*   *steak*   *hotdogs*

B. What does your partner like to eat? What does he or she eat every day? Write five or more affirmative and negative statements about your partner.

   Example   Lydia likes oranges, but she doesn't eat apples.

 GRAMMAR BRIEFING 2

Simple Present Tense—*Wh-* Questions and Answers

WH- QUESTIONS					ANSWERS
WH- QUESTION WORD	DO/DOES	SUBJECT	BASE VERB		
What		I	**need**	for class?	A pen and a notebook.
Where	**do**	you	**live?**		On Center Street.
How often		they	**eat**	there?	Once a week, on Fridays.
What		he	**have**	for lunch?	A sandwich and an apple.
Why	**does**	she	**want**	a computer?	For e-mail.
How often		the class	**meet?**		Three times a week.

 Talking the Talk

1. *What do/does* (somebody) *do?* usually means *What is* (the person's) *job?*

2. *What* or *Where* + *does* sometimes sounds like "What's" or "Where's."

WRITE	YOU WILL OFTEN HEAR
What **does** he do on weekends?	"What's he do on weekends?"
Where **does** she live?	"Where's she live?"

4. Meanings of *Wh-* Questions

A. Match Angie's questions and Zulma's answers.

Angie:

_c_ 1. Where do you go grocery shopping?

____ 2. How often do you shop there?

____ 3. What do you buy there?

____ 4. Why do you shop there?

____ 5. What does he do?

Zulma:

a. Because my brother works there.

b. He's the store manager.

c. At Best Foods supermarket.

d. Once a week.

e. Everything: fruit, vegetables, meat, . . .

B. Work with a partner. Ask and answer the questions in Part A. Take turns.

5. *Wh-* Questions in the Simple Present with *You*

A. Ask your partner about shopping for food. You can use the *wh-* question words and verb phrases in the list. Take turns.

Example   *Student A:* Why do you go to Best Foods Supermarket?

1. where/shop for food
2. why/go
3. how often/go shopping
4. what/buy

Some answers to *How often* questions
once a day
twice a week
three times a month

B. Work in a group. Tell about your partner.

Example   Hector shops for food at Quickmart and Giant Foods. He goes to Quickmart because

it's near his house. He goes one or two times a week. He goes to Giant Foods because

the prices are good. He goes once a week. He buys many things at Giant Foods. At

Quickmart, he buys bread or bananas or candy.

6. *Wh-* Questions in the Simple Present

Write *wh-* questions to ask for the missing information.

1. <u>Where does he live?</u>

2. _____

3. _____

4. _____

5. _____

6. _____

GRAMMAR BRIEFING 3

Adverbs of Frequency

A. MEANINGS OF ADVERBS OF FREQUENCY

100%	always	Ann **always** has breakfast. (all 7 days a week)
	usually	Lou **usually** has breakfast.
	often	Max **often** has breakfast.
	sometimes	Jen **sometimes** has breakfast.
0 %	never	Bill **never** has breakfast. (0 days a week)

B. ADVERBS OF FREQUENCY WITH *BE*

The adverb usually goes AFTER *am/is/are* (+ *not*).

He <u>is</u> **always** hungry.

They <u>aren't</u> **usually** late.

C. ADVERBS OF FREQUENCY WITH OTHER MAIN VERBS

The adverb usually goes BEFORE other main verbs.

She **sometimes** <u>drinks</u> coffee.

He doesn't **always** <u>eat</u> dinner at home.

 Grammar Hotspot!

Never is a negative word. Use only one negative in a statement. Do not use *never* with negative verbs.

He**'s never** at home.
NOT: He ~~isn't~~ never at home.

7. Meanings of Adverbs of Frequency

Look at the schedule with a partner. Who teaches when? Mark statements 1–8 *True* or *False.*
Correct the false statements. Use *always, usually, often, sometimes,* or *never.*

CLASS SCHEDULE	MON.	TUES.	WED.	THURS.	FRI.
8:00–8:50	Ann	Ann	Ann	Ann	—
	Bill	Bill	Bill	Bill	Bill
	Dave	Dave	Dave	Dave	—
9:00–9:50	Ann	—	Ann	—	Ann
	Carly	Carly	Carly	Carly	Carly
	—	Dave	—	Dave	—

        usually

1. Ann ~~always~~ teaches a class at 8:00. *False*

2. Bill always teaches at 8:00.

3. Carly usually teaches at 8:00.

4. Dave always teaches at 8:00.

5. Ann sometimes teaches at 9:00.

6. Bill sometimes teaches at 9:00.

7. Carly sometimes teaches at 9:00.

8. Dave sometimes teaches at 9:00.

8. Word Order with Adverbs of Frequency

A. Put the words in order. Write statements.

1. eat/often/I/in the school cafeteria _____

2. she/breakfast/never/eats _____

3. don't/we/coffee before class/have/always _____

4. usually/don't/you/sugar in your coffee/put _____

5. delicious/the cafeteria food/sometimes/is _____

B. Complete the statements. Write true sentences.

1. I always _____

2. I don't often _____

3. I am usually _____

4. I never _____

5. I'm sometimes _____

6. I don't usually _____

7. I often _____

8. My friends sometimes _____

9. My friends are always _____

10. My friends never _____

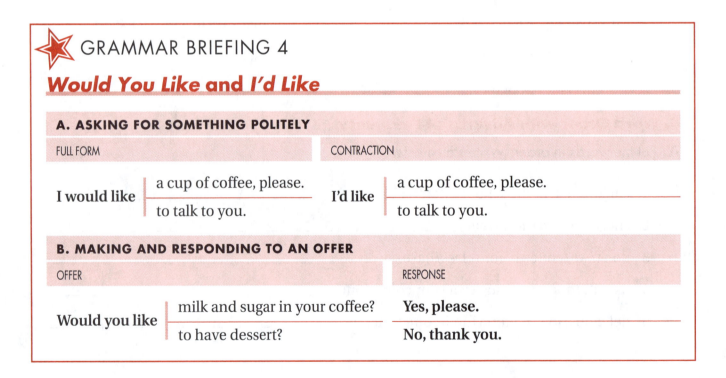

GRAMMAR BRIEFING 4

Would You Like and *I'd Like*

A. ASKING FOR SOMETHING POLITELY

FULL FORM		CONTRACTION	
I would like	a cup of coffee, please.	**I'd like**	a cup of coffee, please.
	to talk to you.		to talk to you.

B. MAKING AND RESPONDING TO AN OFFER

OFFER		RESPONSE
Would you like	milk and sugar in your coffee?	**Yes, please.**
	to have dessert?	**No, thank you.**

💬 Talking the Talk

1. *I would like* means *I want*. Use *I would like* or *I'd like* (+ *please*) to be polite.

Polite

Not polite

2. *Would you like* means *Do you want.* Use *Would you like* to be polite.

Polite: **Would you like** a Coke?

Not as polite: Do you want a Coke?

❾ Polite Offers and Requests

Rewrite the sentences to be more polite.

WANT	WOULD LIKE
1. I want to ask a question.	I'd like to ask a question.
2. *A:* Do you want some help?	_____
B: Yes.	_____
3. Give me a cheeseburger.	_____
4. *A:* Do you want sugar in your coffee?	_____
B: Nope.	_____
5. I want to see the menu.	_____
6. *A:* Do you want to order?	_____
B: Yeah! I want some chicken soup.	_____
7. *A:* Do you want a salad?	_____
B: Yes, and I want Italian dressing on it.	_____

10. Using *I'd Like* and *Would You Like*

A. Look at the pictures with a partner. What are they saying? Write and practice the conversation. Use *I'd like* and *Would you like*.

B. Work alone or with a partner. Write a conversation in a restaurant. Use *I'd like* and *Would you like*.

Waiter/Waitress: _____

Customer: _____

Waiter/Waitress: _____

Customer: _____

Waiter/Waitress: _____

Customer: _____

C. You are sitting at a table in a restaurant. One person in the group is the server (the waiter or waitress). The other people are customers. Act out a conversation.

EXTRA PRACTICE

11. Negative Statements in the Simple Present

Rewrite these sentences as negative statements. Use contractions.

1. I have breakfast every day. _____

2. Rick has lunch in the cafeteria. _____

3. We go out for lunch. _____

4. Molly goes shopping on weekends. _____

5. They eat rice every day. _____

6. I do the dishes after dinner. _____

7. His wife does the cooking. _____

12. *Wh-* Questions in the Simple Present

Put the words in order. Write the *wh-* questions.

1. do/what/eat/you/for breakfast _____

2. you/shop/do/where/for food _____

3. eat/how often/they/do/in restaurants _____

4. those pills/he/does/why/take _____

5. she/for dinner/have/does/what _____

6. how often/coffee/you/do/drink _____

7. does/make/why/he/your lunch _____

8. go/does/where/she/to stop _____

13. *Wh-* Questions in the Simple Present

Write four or more *wh-* questions to ask your teacher. Use *What, Where, Why,* and *How often* + the simple present tense.

Example   *Where do you live?*

14. Adverbs of Frequency

A. Put the words in order. Write statements.

1. always/the cafeteria food/isn't/great _____

2. hungry in class/often/are/we _____

3. get/I/sometimes/hungry in class _____

4. black coffee/usually/drinks/he _____

5. ketchup on French fries/never/puts/she _____

6. isn't/fast food/usually/good for you _____

7. the boys/never/late for dinner/are _____

8. always/has/she/sugar in her tea _____

B. Complete the statements on a piece of paper. Write true sentences.

1. I usually . . . .   4. I never . . . .

2. I am often . . . .   5. I am always . . . .

3. I sometimes . . . .   6. I'm not usually . . . .

Example I usually *eat lunch with Marta and Jenisse.*

15. *Would You Like* and *I'd Like*

Rewrite the sentences to be more polite. Use forms of *would like*.

1. I want some coffee.   _____

2. *A:* Do you want something to drink?   _____

   B: Yeah.   _____

3. I want to ask a question.   _____

4. *A:* Do you want some dessert?   _____

   B: Nope.   _____

5. I want a hamburger with fries.   _____

Unit 4 Wrap-Up Activities

1. Richard's Morning Routine: READING

Read this paragraph.

On most days, Richard goes to work. He has a job at a bank. On work days, Richard gets up at 6:30. He goes to the bathroom, and he shaves. Then he eats a quick breakfast. He usually has cold cereal. Then he brushes his teeth, he combs his hair, and he gets dressed. He always puts on a jacket and tie. At 7:30, he takes the bus to work. On his days off, Richard doesn't go to work. He gets up at 10:00, and he doesn't shave. He puts on a T-shirt and jeans. He often has a big breakfast: juice, eggs, toast, and coffee. He reads the newspaper, and he relaxes. Richard likes his job, but he loves his days off.

2. Morning Routines: WRITING

Interview a classmate. Ask *What do you usually do in the morning? What do you do on your days off?* Take notes. Then write his or her morning routines. Use simple present tense verbs.

3. Lunch: EDITING

Correct the 10 errors in verb forms. The first one is corrected for you.

I ~~am~~ do not always do the same thing for lunch. I'm sometimes eating in the school cafeteria, but I'm usually bring my lunch to school. In the morning, I'm making a sandwich, and I get a piece of fruit. I am not needing a big lunch. My roommate doesn't never make her lunch. She's buy it at school. She dosen't eat much. She always is on a diet. After lunch, I usually study in the library, and she go to class.

4. Find Someone Who: SPEAKING/LISTENING

Step One: Work with a partner. Read statements 1–8. Practice changing them to questions with *Do you* and *Are you* and *Would you like*.

Step Two: Walk around the room. Ask your classmates the questions. Write different names on the lines.

Example *Student A:* Khaled, do you always wear a watch?

1. _____ always wears a watch.

2. _____ is wearing a watch today.

3. _____ uses e-mail.

4. _____ is using a pencil right now.

5. _____ likes Disney movies.

6. _____ would like to visit Disney World.

7. _____ has fun on weekends.

8. _____ would like more homework.

5. The Game 20 Questions: SPEAKING/LISTENING

One student—the Leader—stands in front of the class. He or she thinks of a person but doesn't say the person's name. It can be a famous person, or it can be a person at your school. All the other students take turns asking *yes/no* questions. The Leader can give only *Yes* or *No* answers. The class tries to guess the person. The class can ask no more than twenty questions. (The teacher or another student keeps count of the questions on the blackboard.)

Example Is it a man?   Yes, it is.   Number of questions

Is he famous?   Yes, he is.   / / /

Does he live in this country?   No, he doesn't.

GRAMMAR SUMMARY

Simple Present Tense

AFFIRMATIVE STATEMENTS

I/We/You/They **work.**   He/She/It **works.**

NEGATIVE STATEMENTS

I/We/You/They | **do not work.**   He/She/It | **does not work.**
              | **don't work.** | **doesn't work.**

YES/NO QUESTIONS AND SHORT ANSWERS

QUESTIONS	SHORT ANSWERS
Do I/we/you/they **need** help?	Yes, I/we/you/they **do.**
	No, I/we/you/they **don't.**
Does he/she/it **need** help?	Yes, he/she/it **does.**
	No, he/she/it **doesn't.**

WH- QUESTIONS AND ANSWERS

QUESTIONS	ANSWERS
What do you **have** for breakfast?	Juice, toast, and coffee.
How often does she **see** movies?	Every weekend.

★ See the Grammar Briefings on pages 114, 116, 121, 131, and 133.

Spelling of Simple Present Third Person Singular Verbs

BASE VERB	THIRD PERSON SINGULAR
play	play**s**
wash	wash**es**
study	stud**ies**

★ See the Grammar Briefing on page 116. See also Appendix 6 on page A-6.

Present Progressive vs. Simple Present

CORRECT	NOT CORRECT
He's **taking** a test right now.	**NOT:** He ~~takes~~ a test right now.
She **takes** the bus every day.	**NOT:** She ~~'s taking~~ the bus every day.
Does he **want/like/need/know** it?	**NOT:** ~~Is he wanting/liking/needing/ knowing~~ it?

★ See the Grammar Briefing on page 124.

Adverbs of Frequency

WITH *BE*	WITH OTHER VERBS

He | is | always / often / never | on my bus.

He | always / often / never | takes | the #42 bus.

★ See the Grammar Briefing on page 136.

Would You Like/I'd Like

REQUESTS

I **would like** / I**'d like** | some coffee, please.

OFFERS

OFFER	RESPONSES
Would you like sugar in your coffee?	**Yes, please.**
	No, thank you.

★ See the Grammar Briefing on page 138.

TEST YOURSELF ON CHAPTER 7

1. Complete the paragraph. Use the simple present tense.

   Rafael is a pilot. He _____ for Atlantic Airlines. He _____ big airplanes for this
                       1 (work)   2 (fly)

   company. The planes _____ 300 people. Rafael always _____, "I _____
                       3 (carry)   4 (say)   5 (love)

   my job." Every week, he _____ to London and Paris. He _____ friends there.
                      6 (go)   7 (have)

   They always _____ a good time together, but he _____ his family.
                   8 (have)   9 (miss)

2. Write the third person singular form of the simple present tense.

   1. talk   _talks_   4. play _____   7. put on _____

   2. carry _____   5. kiss _____   8. finish _____

   3. watch _____   6. marry _____   9. cry _____

3. Change each statement to a *yes/no* question and short answer.

   1. I don't like ketchup.   _Do you like ketchup?_____   _No, I don't._

   2. She cooks Chinese food. _____ _____

   3. They don't eat meat. _____ _____

   4. The soup doesn't need salt. _____ _____

   5. He washes the dishes. _____ _____

4. Write the correct tense of the verb. Use simple present or present progressive.

   1. (ring) The phone _____. Can you get it?

   2. (know) I _____ the answer!

   3. (not, listen) The bus driver is speaking, but the people on the bus _____.

   4. (need) You _____ a new toothbrush.

5. Find the six errors and correct them.

   1. The store ~~sell~~ many kinds of food.   4. We're do our homework at the library.
           sells

   2. I'm liking my classmates.   5. He's work at the mall.

   3. Does he takes the bus every day?   6. Are you have a car?

TEST YOURSELF ON CHAPTER 8

6. Make the sentences negative. Use contractions.

1. We have class on Saturdays. _We don't have class on Saturdays._ _____

2. He enjoys parties. _____

3. The flowers need more water. _____

4. She has a lot of homework. _____

5. You listen to me. _____

7. Write *wh-* questions to match the answers.

1. _Where do you live?_ _____   I live in Springfield.

2. _____   He has class three times a week.

3. _____   I'm a mechanic. I fix cars.

4. _____   They work at Mercy Hospital.

8. Rewrite each statement. Add the adverb of frequency in parentheses ( ).

1. (always) The bus doesn't come on time. _____

2. (usually) I am on time. _____

3. (often) Tom doesn't get up early. _____

4. (never) She calls me. _____

9. Rewrite the conversation. Use a form of *would like.*

A: Do you want something to drink?   *A:* _____

B: Yes, please. I want some coffee.   *B:* _____

A: Do you want cream and sugar in it?   *A:* _____

B: I want just milk, please.   *B:* _____

10. Find the six errors and correct them.

1. That restaurant ~~don't~~ *doesn't* serve pizza.

2. Where is he usually eat lunch?

3. We don't never eat in nice restaurants.

4. How often you eat ice cream?

5. I like some more water, please.

6. She doesn't has a car.   See Answer Key pages ANS-4 and ANS-5.

Going Places

Chapter 9
It's Sunny and Warm

- Telling the time, day, date, and weather with *It's*
- Prepositional phrases
- Prepositions for describing time
- Prepositions for describing location or place
- Object pronouns

Chapter 10
Eating Out

- Count and noncount nouns
- The indefinite article *a/an*
- The definite article *the*
- Questions with *Is there/Are there*
- Quantifiers *many/much, a lot of, some/any, a little/a few*
- Questions with *How many* and *How much*

9 It's Sunny and Warm

GRAMMAR IN ACTION

Reading and Listening

A. Listen and read.

Narrator: Yuki and Kazumi are at the airport. They see their friend Manuel. He's waiting in line. They're surprised to see him, and he's surprised to see them.

Yuki: Look who's in front of us!

Kazumi: Manuel! Hello! Where are you going?

Manuel: Hi! I'm going to Puerto Rico, to see my mother. I always visit her in December.

Yuki: Yeah, when it gets cold and snowy around here . . .

Manuel: . . . and it's sunny and warm down there!

Kazumi: Where does your mother live?

Manuel: In Bayamón. It's near San Juan. And what about you? What are you doing at the airport?

Yuki: We're going to Mexico.

Kazumi: For a week at the beach!

Manuel: That sounds great. Have fun!

B. Form a group of three. Practice the conversation in Part A.

Think about Grammar

A. Circle the correct word from the conversation. Write it on the line. Answer the question.

1. *Narrator:* They're surprised to see (he/**him**).

   Who does the word " _him_ " refer to in this sentence?   _Manuel_

2. *Narrator:* . . . and he's surprised to see (they/them).

   Who does the word "_____" refer to in this sentence?   _____

3. *Yuki:* Look who's in front of (we/us)!

   Who does the word "_____" refer to in this sentence?   _____

4. *Manuel:* I always visit (she/her) in December.

   Who does the word "_____" refer to in this sentence?   _____

B. The words in the box come from the conversation. Write them in the chart.

at the airport	cold and snowy	sunny and warm
in December	for a week	near San Juan

TIME	WEATHER	PLACE/LOCATION

C. Do you know more words for time, weather, or places? Add them to the chart.

GRAMMAR BRIEFING 1

It + the Time, Day, Date, or Weather

A. TELLING TIME

QUESTION	ANSWERS
	IT + IS
What time is it?	**It is** six o'clock.
	It's 6:00.

See page 8 for more about telling time.

B. TELLING THE DAY

QUESTION	ANSWERS
	IT + IS
What day is it?	**It is** Monday.
	It's

See Appendix 2 for the days of the week and their abbreviations.

C. TELLING THE DATE

QUESTION	ANSWERS
	IT + IS
What's the date?	**It is** January 1, 2005. ("January first, two thousand five.")
	It's March 22. ("March twenty-second.")

See Appendix 1 for ordinal numbers and Appendix 2 for more about telling the date.

D. DESCRIBING THE WEATHER

QUESTION	ANSWERS	
	IT + IS	VERB + -ING
	It is	raining.
	It's	snowing.
How's the weather?	IT + IS	ADJECTIVE
What's the weather like?	**It is**	hot/warm/cool/cold.
	It's	windy/rainy/snowy.
		sunny/cloudy.

Grammar Hotspot!

It's and *its* sound the same, but they are different:

- *It's = It is.*
- *Its* is a possessive adjective.

The car is hot. **Its** windows are closed, and **it's** sunny today.

It's 11:00 A.M./Tuesday/May 1.
   NOT: ~~Its~~ 11:00 A.M./Tuesday/May 1.

1. Statements about the Time/Day/Weather

Write statements with *It's.*

1. | 4:00 | It's four o'clock. _____

2. | 8:00 | _____

3. | 12:00 | _____

4. What day is it? ___It's_ Th _ursday._____

5. What day is it? _____ W_____

6. What day is it? _____F_____

7. _____   8. _____   9. _____

2. Error Correction

Correct the statements.

            It's
1. ~~Is~~ raining.

2. Its sunny.

3. The weather is snowing.

4. How's the weather like?

5. Its Tuesday.

6. It's clouds today.

7. It cool and cloudy.

8. Is warm today.

9. Its two o'clock.

10. What the time?

11. What day it is?

12. Today Monday.

13. It's 5:00 o'clock.

14. Its snowing.

15. It's 15 March.

3. Dates

Work with a partner. Write the dates. Say the dates. (Note: The order is month/day/year.)

Example *Write:* It's January 1, 2005.   *Say:* It's January first, two thousand five.

1. 1/1/2005 _____
2. 2/2/2006 _____
3. 10/20/2008 _____
4. 5/13/2010 _____
5. 8/24/2011 _____

6. 4/30/2012 _____
7. 7/15/2015 _____
8. 3/10/2020 _____
9. 6/21/2033 _____
10. 9/12/2099 _____

4. Talking about the Time and the Weather

🎧

A. Look at the pictures. Listen to the conversation. Who is talking? Choose picture 1, 2, or 3.

1. New York City 5:00 P.M.   2. Florida 3:00 P.M.   3. Seattle, Washington 8:00 A.M.

California 2:00 P.M.

Colorado 1:00 P.M.

Montreal, Canada 11:00 A.M.

B. The people in pictures 1, 2, and 3 are all talking about the time and the weather. What are they saying? Work with a partner to act out their conversations.

GRAMMAR BRIEFING 2

Prepositional Phrases; Prepositions for Describing Time

A. PREPOSITIONS AND PREPOSITIONAL PHRASES

1. A **preposition** can be one word, two, or three.

in	on	before	after
from	to	next to	in front of

2. A preposition takes an **object**.

> preposition + object
> The game begins **at   noon.**

It can have more than one object.

> preposition + objects
> I have classes **with   Julio, Niko, and Hiro.**

3. A preposition + its object = a **prepositional phrase.**

> prepositional phrases
> What do you do <u>in the morning</u> <u>before school</u>?

4. A preposition links its object with another part of the sentence.

> **Ann** is **in** her **room.**

B. PREPOSITIONS FOR DESCRIBING TIME

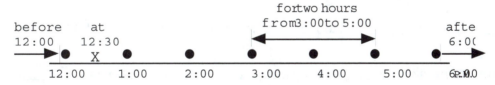

I get to school a little **before** 12:00. My first class starts **at** 12:30. My second class goes **from** 3:00 **to** 5:00. The class lasts **for** two hours. **After** 6:00, I meet my friends.

Grammar Hotspot!

1. Use *on* + a day.

> We don't have classes **on Saturday** or **Sunday.**

2. Use *in* + a month or a season.

> The school year ends **in June.**
> We go to the beach **in the summer.**

3. Use *in* + *the morning, the afternoon,* or *the evening,* BUT use *at* + *night.*

> I get up at 7:00 **in the morning.**
> I go to bed at 11:30 **at night.**

5. Identifying Prepositions and Their Objects

Circle the 14 prepositions. The first one is done for you. Underline the objects of the prepositions. The first one is done for you.

Cathy works (at) <u>a candle factory</u>. She makes candles in different colors, sizes, and shapes. They have many different smells, too. She works on Tuesdays, Wednesdays, Thursdays, Fridays, and Saturdays. She starts at 7:00 in the morning. She has lunch from 11:00 to 12:00. Sometimes she eats her lunch in the park next to the factory. She and a friend often take a walk after lunch. Her shift ends at 3:00 in the afternoon. Cathy takes a vacation in the summer. Her family goes to the beach.

a factory

candles

6. Prepositions for Describing Time

Use the prepositions *after, at, for, from, in, on,* and *to.*

Robert works at a convenience store. Convenience stores are almost always open.

Robert works there _____ night. His shift lasts _____ eight hours. He works
                           1   2

_____ 11:00 P.M. _____ 7:00 A.M. He closes the store _____ 3:00 and takes
  3   4   5

a 15-minute break. _____ the morning, he goes out for breakfast _____ work.
                    6   7

Then he goes home, and he sleeps _____ six or seven hours. _____ the afternoon,
                             8   9

he sometimes goes to the gym. He takes classes _____ the evening. Robert works
                                            10

five nights a week. He doesn't work _____ weekends.
                                  11

He's planning to take a vacation _____ January. He likes
                              12

to go on vacation _____ the winter. This year, he wants
                      13

to go Las Vegas _____ a week.
                 14

7. Prepositions for Describing Time

Look at the diagram of Ed's daily schedule. Write statements to answer the questions. Use *after*, *at*, *before*, *for*, *from*, and *to*.

```
              9:00              12:00              5:00
go to the gym ➜ ●─────────────────●─────────────────●─➜ see his girlfrien
            start work        have lunch        finish work
```

1. How many hours does Ed work each day? *Ed works for eight hours each day.* _____

2. When does he work? _____

3. When does he go to the gym? _____

4. What time does he have lunch? _____

5. When does he see his girlfriend? _____

8. Talking about Time

A. Work with a partner to write five questions with *What time* and *When*.

    Examples   *What time do you get up?*

                     When do you see your friends?

QUESTIONS	_____'S ANSWERS
	(Name)
1. _____	_____
2. _____	_____
3. _____	_____
4. _____	_____
5. _____	_____

B. Find a new partner. Ask your questions and write his or her answers.

GRAMMAR BRIEFING 3

Prepositions for Describing Location or Place

Ms. Hall works **in** the bank.

The bank is **next to** the post office.

It's **between** the post office and the deli, **across from** the fire station.

Ramiro always sits **near** Cristina and Tai-Hung.

He sits **in back of** Cristina. He sits **in front of** Tai-Hung.

His books are usually **on** his desk. His backpack stays **under** his chair.

 Grammar Hotspot!

1. Use *in* + a city, state, country, or continent.	He lives **in** Miami. Miami is **in** Florida/**in** the United States/**in** North America.
2. Use *on* + a street or floor.	They live **on** Main Street. Their apartment is **on** the third floor.
3. Use *at* + a building or a specific address.	She works **at** the bank. It's **at** 11 Main St.

9. Prepositions for Describing Location or Place

A. Look at the picture. The Johnsons are on vacation. They're staying at a hotel near the beach. Listen to the statements, and circle True or False.

1. (True) False   3. True False   5. True False   7. True False   9. True False

2. True False   4. True False   6. True False   8. True False   10. True False

B. Work with a partner. Look at the picture in Part A. Take turns to complete and say statements 1–10 below. Make two more statements with prepositions.

1. The Johnsons are staying at . . .

2. Seaside is in . . .

3. New Jersey is in . . .

4. The Johnsons' hotel is on . . .

5. Green Street is between . . . and . . .

6. The hotel is . . .

7. Room 321 is on . . .

8. There's a . . . across from the hotel.

9. The hotel is next to . . .

10. The Johnson's can eat at . . .

11. _____

12. _____

C. Write about the place where you live.

1. I live in _____

2. I live on _____

3. I live at _____

10. Prepositions for Describing Location or Place

A. Work with a partner. Look at picture A. The videotapes on these shelves have no titles on them. Which one is which? Read the clues. Write the titles on the tapes.

CLUES

1. *Titanic* is in front of *E.T.*
2. *Tango* is between *Die Hard* and *Gandhi*.
3. *Jurassic Park* is between *Die Hard* and *Supercop*.
4. *Gandhi* is next to *Tango* and under *Cinderella*.
5. *Jaws* is in back of *Cinderella*.

A.    B.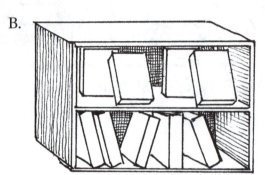

B. Student A: Use picture B. Write these new titles (but don't show your partner!): *Star Wars, Rocky, Love Story, The Matrix, Bambi, Spiderman, The Godfather,* and *King Kong*. Give clues to the locations of the tapes. Use prepositions. Student B: Listen, write the clues, and mark the titles on the tapes. Take turns.

11. Prepositions for Describing Location or Place

Look at the people and things in your classroom. Student A: Ask questions with *Where*. Student B: Use prepositions in your answers. Take turns.

Example   *Student A:* Where is Normando?

   Student B: He's sitting in front of Jong-Su.

GRAMMAR BRIEFING 4

Object Pronouns

A. SUBJECT PRONOUNS AND OBJECT PRONOUNS

SUBJECT PRONOUNS	OBJECT PRONOUNS	
I	**me**	She loves **me.**
we	**us**	He's calling **us.**
you	**you**	I'm talking to **you.**
he	**him**	She sits next to **him.**
she	**her**	He lives with **her.**
it	**it**	They're buying **it.**
they	**them**	I like **them.**

B. USING OBJECT PRONOUNS

1. Use object pronouns after verbs.	She **likes him.**
2. Use object pronouns after prepositions.	Please speak **to them.**

Talking the Talk

1. Do not say *me and* (another person). Use (another person) *and me.*	Please wait for George and me. **NOT:** Please wait for ~~me and George~~.
2. Use (another person) *and me* only after a verb or after a preposition. Use (another person) *and I* as the subject of a verb.	George and I have class at 2:00. **NOT:** ~~Me and George~~ have class at 2:00.

12. Object Pronouns after Verbs

A. Write the object form of the boldfaced pronoun.

1. **I** can see you, and you can see __me__ .

2. **He** loves her, and she loves _____ .

3. **We** like them, and they like _____ .

4. **You** help me, and I help _____ .

5. **They** know me, and I know _____ .

6. **She** calls me, and I call _____ .

7. **I** help him, and he helps _____ .

8. **He** knows us, and we know _____ .

B. Write the pronoun that refers to the boldfaced word.

1. I don't like **cats,** but he loves _____ .

2. I don't eat **pizza,** but he loves _____ .

3. He doesn't drink **milk,** but I drink _____ every day.

4. He likes **dogs,** but I hate _____ .

5. I rent **videos**, but he buys _____ .

6. I love **the beach,** but he doesn't like _____ at all.

13. Object Pronouns after Prepositions

Work in a group. Student A: Point to someone in the room and ask a question. Use *Who's sitting* + a preposition (*next to, in front of, in back of, near*) + an object pronoun. Take turns.

Example   *Student A* (pointing at a student): Who's sitting next to her?

   Students B and C: Ahmed and Thuy.

   Student B: Who's sitting in back of me?

   Students A and C: Nelly.

14. Using (Another Person) *and I/Me*

A. Correct the errors.

1. Hiro and me work together.

2. Wait for Lazar and I.

3. Me and my boyfriend like to dance.

4. Saad and me play tennis.

5. Me and Rina have class now.

6. My children help my husband and I.

B. Work with a partner. Make true statements. Use (name) *and I* or (name) *and me.*

Examples   *Student A:* My boyfriend and I talk on the phone every day.

   Student B: Ayako eats lunch with Natsumi and me.

EXTRA PRACTICE

15. Using *It's* + the Time, Day, Date, or Weather

Use *It's* in statements about the time now, the day, the date, and the weather.

1. What time is it? _____

2. What day is it? _____

3. What's the date today? _____

4. What's the weather like? _____

16. Prepositions for Describing Time; Prepositional Phrases

A. Write the prepositions *after, at, before, for, from, in,* and *to.*

Cathy is on vacation. Her family goes to the beach every year _____ the
₁

summer. They stay _____ two weeks. Cathy loves it. She gets up _____
₂   ₃

9:00 or 10:00 _____ the morning. _____ noon _____ 5:00,
₄   ₅   ₆

she's in the water or on the beach. Sometimes she sleeps on the beach _____
₇

an hour or two. She always sleeps well _____ night. These two weeks are
₈

wonderful. _____ her vacation, Cathy feels tired. _____ her vacation,
₉   ₁₀

she feels great.

B. Underline the 15 prepositional phrases in Part A.

Example Cathy is <u>on vacation</u>. Her family goes <u>to the beach</u>. . . .

17. Prepositions for Describing Place or Location

Look at the picture of the teacher's desk on page 32. On a piece of paper, write eight statements about things on the desk. Use the prepositions *in, on, near, in front of, in back of, under, between,* and *next to.*

Examples There are many things on the teacher's desk.

               The teacher has some flowers in a cup.

18. Prepositions for Describing Place or Location

Look at the picture of the street on page 158. Answer the questions below with one or more prepositional phrases.

1. Where is the gas station? _across from the deli, next to the fire station_ _____

2. Where is the fire station? _____

3. Where is the park? _____

4. Where is the deli? _____

5. Where is the post office? _____

6. Where is the bank? _____

19. Object Pronouns

Write the object pronoun that refers to the boldfaced word.

1. **I** sit next to you, and you sit next to _me_____ .

2. He doesn't like **the beach,** but she loves _____ .

3. I can see him, and he can see _____ .

4. **You** write to me, and I write to _____ .

5. **He** loves her, and she loves _____ , too.

6. Sometimes **she** helps me with homework, and sometimes I help _____ .

7. I never eat **vegetables,** but he loves _____ .

8. **We** know them, and they know _____ .

9. **My friends** trust me, and I trust _____ .

10. I don't take **the bus,** but he takes _____ every day.

11. Yes, I know **George.** Everybody knows _____ .

12. Do you like **Julia?** I like _____ .

GRAMMAR IN ACTION

Reading and Listening

A. Listen and read.

Narrator: Yuki and Kazumi are at the beach in Mexico.

Kazumi: Are you hungry? Remember, we have a bag of food.

Yuki: I'm starving! What's in the bag?

Kazumi: Well, there's bread and fruit . . .

Yuki: Are there any grapes?

Kazumi: No, we don't have any grapes, but there's watermelon, and we have two oranges.

Yuki: The watermelon sounds good. Is there any meat or cheese? To make sandwiches?

Kazumi: We have meat *AND* cheese . . .

Yuki: What kind?

Kazumi: The meat is chicken, and the cheese is . . . I don't know! And we have lettuce and tomatoes, too.

Yuki: Terrific! How many sandwiches can we make?

Kazumi: How much food do you need?!

Yuki: A lot! I always get hungry at the beach.

B. Work with a partner. Practice the conversation in Part A.

Think about Grammar

A. Circle the article *a, the,* or — (no article) in these sentences from the conversation.

1. a. *Kazumi:* Remember, we have (a/the/—) **bag** of food.

   b. *Yuki:* What's in (a/the/—) **bag**?

2. a. *Kazumi:* No, there aren't any grapes, but there's (a/the/—) **watermelon** . . .

   b. *Yuki:* (A/The/—) **watermelon** sounds good.

3. a. *Kazumi:* We have (a/the/—) **meat** AND (a/the/—) **cheese** . . .

   b. *Kazumi:* (A/The/—) **meat** is chicken, and (a/the/—) **cheese** is . . .

Look at sentences 1.b, 2.b, and 3.b. The nouns *bag, watermelon, meat,* and *cheese* are repeated. What article comes before the nouns when they are repeated? _____

B. Find the eleven words for food in the conversation. Four are plural count nouns. Seven are noncount nouns; they do not end in *-s*. Write them all in the chart.

PLURAL COUNT NOUNS	NONCOUNT NOUNS
grapes	bread

C. Work with a partner. Can you name the foods in the pictures? Write the words in the chart.

PLURAL COUNT NOUNS	NONCOUNT NOUNS

GRAMMAR BRIEFING 1

Count and Noncount Nouns; The Indefinite Article *A/An*

A. COUNT NOUNS

1. **Count nouns** name people, places, and things that we can count (1, 2, 3. . .).

SINGULAR	PLURAL
one book	two books

2. Remember: Use a singular verb after a singular subject noun and a plural verb after a plural subject noun.

Your **friend is** here.

Your **friends are** here.

B. NONCOUNT NOUNS

1. **Noncount nouns** name things that we cannot count. They do not have singular and plural forms; they have one form only. Some common noncount nouns are:

FOOD		LIQUIDS		OTHER	
bread	meat	coffee	oil	advice	information
butter	rice	gas(oline)	soda	air	mail
cheese	salt	juice	tea	fun	music
fruit	sugar	milk	water	gold	traffic
				ice	work

See Appendix 4 for more examples of noncount nouns.

2. Many noncount nouns name groups of countable things.

NONCOUNT	COUNTABLE
furniture	one table, two chairs, a bed
money	a dollar, two quarters, many coins

3. Noncount noun subjects take singular verbs.

This music **is** great.

The water **feels** cold.

C. INDEFINITE ARTICLES

1. The **indefinite article** *a* or *an* can come before a singular count noun. The noun is not specific.

Would you like **a cookie?** (not one specific cookie—any cookie)

Would you like **an apple?** (not one specific apple—any apple)

2. Use no article before a plural count noun that is not specific.

I like **apples.** (any and all apples—apples in general)

3. Use no article before a noncount noun that is not specific.

Would you like **sugar** in your coffee? (not specific sugar—any sugar)

 ## Grammar Hotspot!

Do not use *a, an,* or a number before a noncount noun. Do not add *-s* to a noncount noun.

I eat bread every day.
 NOT: I eat ~~a~~ bread every day.

I'd like two pieces of bread.
 NOT: I'd like two ~~breads~~.

1. Singular and Plural Count Nouns vs. Noncount Nouns

Write the plural form of the noun or write *noncount.*

1. desk   <u>desks</u>
2. furniture <u>noncount</u>
3. guitar   _____
4. music   _____
5. work   _____

6. homework _____
7. dish   _____
8. traffic   _____
9. dollar   _____
10. gold   _____

11. mail   _____
12. letter   _____
13. air   _____
14. cloud   _____
15. rice   _____

2. Indefinite Articles + Nouns

Write *a, an,* or — (no article).

1. Do I have ____ mail?

2. The class has ____ new teacher.

3. Do you eat ____ meat?

4. He grows ____ apples on his farm.

5. They want ____ information.

6. Do you have ____ umbrella?

7. My car needs ____ gas.

8. They build ____ beautiful houses.

9. You need ____ advice from a doctor.

10. She's not wearing ____ jewelry.

11. They always have ____ fun there.

12. Here is ____ chair for you.

13. I like to go to ____ nice stores.

14. He's eating ____ orange.

15. Do you cook with ____ oil or butter?

16. You need ____ warm hat.

3. Subject Nouns and Singular/Plural Verbs

A. Circle the correct verb.

Nancy is telling her friends to come into the kitchen.

Nancy's refrigerator

Nancy: Hey, everybody! Come and eat—the food (1. is/are)
on the table!

Bill: Wow, all this food (2. look/looks) great.

Nancy: The drinks (3. is/are) in the refrigerator. The milk

(4. is/are) on the top shelf. The orange juice (5. is/are)

next to the milk, and there (6. is/are) soda on the bottom shelf. The soda cans

(7. is/are) cold, I think, but there (8. is/are) ice in the freezer if you want it. The

iced tea (9. has/have) lemon but no sugar in it—the sugar (10. is/are) on the

table. I can make coffee, too.

Dan: Ahh, coffee! That (11. sound/sounds) good. Thanks.

B. Listen to the conversation in Part A. Check your answers.

GRAMMAR BRIEFING 2

The Definite Article *The*

USING *THE*

1. Use *the* when you use a noun for the second time.	**1** **2**
2. Use *the* when you and your listener both know the noun.	*Al:* Where's **the** dog? *Sara:* In **the** kitchen. (He is speaking about one specific dog, and she knows the dog. She is speaking about one specific kitchen, and he knows the kitchen.)
3. *The* can come before singular, plural, and noncount nouns.	**The sun** is shining. **The clouds** are small and white. **The weather** is fine today.

 Grammar Hotspot!

1. Use *the* for specific people, places, and things.

COUNT NOUNS		NONCOUNT NOUNS
SINGULAR	PLURAL	
the	the	the

The flowers in your yard are beautiful. (I mean those flowers only.)

I like **the music** on that CD. (I mean that specific music.)

2. Use *a, an,* or no article when the noun is not specific.

COUNT NOUNS		NONCOUNT NOUNS
SINGULAR	PLURAL	
a/an	—	—

I love **flowers.** (I love all flowers, flowers in general.)
NOT: I love ~~the~~ flowers.

Music is important to me. (Music in general is important to me.)
NOT: ~~The~~ music is important to me.

4. Reasons for Using *The*

A. Work with a partner. Read the telephone conversation in Part B.

B. Why do the speakers use *the* before the boldfaced nouns? Check (✓) your answers in the chart.

	IT'S THE SECOND USE OF THE NOUN.	BOTH PEOPLE KNOW THE NOUN.
1.		
2.		
3.		
4.		
5.		
6.		
7.		
8.		

Mother: How's **the weather** there?
1

Son: Great! **The sun** is shining, and
2

there's not a cloud in **the sky.**
3

Mother: Nice! Do you have plans for **the day?**
4

Son: Yup—a soccer game and then a party.

Mother: Where is **the game?**
5

Son: At **the new stadium.**
6

Mother: And where's **the party?**
7

Son: It's a picnic by **the river.**
8

5. Definite and Indefinite Articles

Complete the sentences in this e-mail message. Write *a, an, the,* or — (no article).

Hi Mira! How are you? Everything here is fine, especially __the__ weather. Today is
1

_____ BEAUTIFUL day! _____ sun is shining and _____ temperature is about 75°.
2   3   4

All my friends are at _____ picnic by the river, but I have _____ work to do,
5   6

LOTS of work. I have _____ book to read for history, and _____ papers to
7   8

write, and _____ verbs to study for Spanish. Maybe I can take _____ history book
9   10

outside and read it under _____ tree. I can study _____ verbs outside, too. But I
11   12

can't write _____ papers outside. Write to me! Love, Nikki
13

6. Definite and Indefinite Articles

Work in a group. Look at the picture. What is wrong? Make statements with *a/an/the/*(no article) + noun.

⭐ GRAMMAR BRIEFING 3

Questions with *Is There/Are There*

QUESTIONS			SHORT ANSWERS
IS THERE	SINGULAR COUNT NOUN		
	a **mall**	near here?	Yes, there **is.**
Is there	NONCOUNT NOUN		No, there **isn't.**
	heavy **traffic**	on this road?	
ARE THERE	PLURAL COUNT NOUN		
			Yes, there **are.**
Are there	good **restaurants**	at the mall?	No, there **aren't.**

USING *IS/ARE THERE* QUESTIONS

Questions with *Is there* or *Are there* often ask about a time or place.

Is there a movie at 8:00?

Are there many cars on the street?

💬 Talking the Talk

There, their, and *they're* all sound the same. They have the same pronunciation but different meanings.

> **There** is a movie theater near here.
> (*there + be*)
>
> My friends have **their** tickets for the 7:00 movie. (possessive adjective)
>
> **They're** waiting in front of the theater. (*they + are*)

7. *There, Their,* and *They're*

Complete the sentences. Write *there, their,* or *they're.*

Rosalie and Sandra work at a restaurant. It's a family restaurant. (1) __Their__ mother and father own it, and (2) _____ brothers work there, too. The family works hard, and (3) _____ restaurant is very successful. Rosalie and Sandra are waitresses there. In the evening, (4) _____ always busy. (5) _____ is a big crowd of customers every night. These people come for the good Mexican food. (6) _____ are many different Mexican dishes on the menu. (7) _____ all delicious! Right now it's 7:00 P.M. and (8) _____ are people at all the tables. (9) _____ is a line of people outside the door, too! (10) _____ hungry.

8. Questions with *Is There/Are There*

A. Student A: Look at the picture on page 176 and listen. Student B: Ask about the picture. Use *Is there* or *Are there* + the words in the box.

Example *Student B:* Is there a waiter in the picture?
         Student A: Yes, there is.

1. a waiter/in the picture	4. food/on the tables
2. a clock/on the wall	5. flowers/on the tables
3. children/in the restaurant	6. music/in the restaurant

B. Student A: Ask the questions. Student B: Look at page 176.

1. two people/at the table in the middle	4. two coffee cups/next to their plates
2. plates of food/in front of them	5. bread/on the table
3. fish/on their plates	6. money/on the table

 GRAMMAR BRIEFING 4

Quantifiers *Many, Much, A Lot Of, Some, Any, A Few, A Little;* Questions with *How Many/How Much*

A. QUANTIFIERS

Quantifiers can come before nouns. Quantifiers tell how many or how much.

BEFORE PLURAL NOUNS

many
—————— grapes
a lot of

some
—————— grapes
any

a few grapes

BEFORE NONCOUNT NOUNS

much
—————— fruit
a lot of

some
—————— fruit
any

a little fruit

B. QUESTIONS WITH *HOW MANY/HOW MUCH*

1. Use *How many* + plural noun.

> **How many eggs** do we have?

2. Use *How much* + noncount noun.

> **How much soda** is in the refrigerator?

☀ Grammar Hotspot!

1. Use *a lot of,* not *much,* in affirmative statements.	He drinks **a lot of** soda. **NOT:** He drinks ~~much~~ soda.
2. Use *some* in affirmative statements and *any* in negative statements.	We **have some** salt, but we **don't have any** pepper.

9. Quantifiers with Count and Noncount Nouns

A. Circle the correct words.

1. I'd like (a few/a little) more coffee, please.

2. There are only (a few/a little) strawberries.

3. I like (a few/a little) butter on my bread.

4. There's (a few/a little) lettuce for salad.

5. *A:* Do you eat eggs?

   B: Yes, but (not many/not much).

6. *A:* Do we have any cheese?

   B: Yes, but (not many/not much).

B. Write *many, much,* or *a lot of.* Write two quantifiers when you can.

1. He doesn't have _much/a lot of_ money.

2. I have _a lot of_ homework.

3. They eat _____ ice cream.

4. Are there _____ bananas?

5. You don't use _____ oil.

6. He puts _____ salt on his food.

7. She doesn't like _____ vegetables.

8. There's _____ sugar in this tea.

C. Write *some* or *any.* Write both quantifiers when you can.

1. We don't need _any_ bread.

2. Are there _some/any_ oranges?

3. I'd like _____ watermelon.

4. Do we have _____ cheese?

5. She never eats _____ desserts.

6. Are they buying _____ fish?

10. Questions with *How Much/How Many;* Quantifiers

A. Listen to the conversation. Check (✓) the things the nurse asks about.

	QUESTIONS	ANSWERS	QUESTIONS	ANSWERS
✓	coffee	a lot	fish	
	tea		vegetables	
	water		fruit	
	soda		meat	
	eggs		cigarettes	

B. Listen again. Write quantifiers in the chart for Mr. Feldman's answers.

C. Student A is a doctor or nurse, and Student B is a patient. Student A: Ask questions with *How many* or *How much.* Student B: Give your answers. Take turns.

11. Questions with Quantifiers

Work with a partner. Ask and answer questions about the picture. Use *Is/Are there any/much/many* + nouns (such as *people, food, furniture, animals, money*). Take turns.

Example   *Student A:* Are there any children in the picture?

         Student B: No, there aren't.

EXTRA PRACTICE

12. Indefinite Articles

Write *a*, *an*, or — (no article).

1. That movie is not for ___ children.
2. Sheree has ___ job for the summer.
3. You can get ___ information online.
4. Do we have ___ homework tonight?
5. I need ___ eraser.
6. They listen to ___ music all the time.
7. I'm thirsty. I need ___ water.
8. There's ___ orange on the table.
9. I often have ___ banana for breakfast.
10. We're asking them for ___ advice.
11. Are you having ___ fun?
12. I know ___ people in your class.
13. Would you like ___ ice in your glass?
14. He wears ___ hat at the beach.
15. Let's get ___ drinks at the café.
16. In that store, ___ meat is expensive.
17. I see ___ airplane in the sky.
18. They're asking for ___ money.

13. The Definite Article *The* and the Indefinite Articles *A/An*, and —

Look at the picture of the restaurant on page 172. Write eight statements about it on a piece of paper. Use the article in parentheses (or no article) + noun.

1. (a)
2. (a)
3. (an)
4. (the)
5. (the)
6. (—)
7. (—)
8. (—)

Example 1. There is a clock on the wall.

14. *There, Their, and They're*

Write *there, their,* or *they're.*

Denis and Rita need to go grocery shopping. (1) _____ going to the supermarket. (2) _____ favorite supermarket is Best Foods Market. It has good vegetables and fruit. (3) _____ always fresh. (4) _____ are good prices at this store, too. It's not expensive. Denis and Rita are taking (5) _____ children with them. (6) _____ little boy and girl help them shop. (7) _____ happy to go to the supermarket. They get (8) _____ favorite cookies and ice cream there. Today, (9) _____ are a lot of people at the supermarket. (10) _____ shopping today because it's Saturday.

15. Quantifiers with Count and Noncount Nouns

A. Write *a little* or *a few.*

1. He's on vacation for _____ days.

2. I'd like _____ butter, please.

3. I have only _____ homework.

4. I know _____ people in India.

B. Write *many, much,* or *a lot of.* Write two quantifiers when you can.

1. We eat _____ rice.

2. Is there _____ cheese on the pizza?

3. I don't send _____ letters.

4. There is _____ mail for you.

C. Write *some* or *any.* Write both quantifiers when you can.

1. The car doesn't have _____ gas.

2. Is there _____ milk?

3. Please buy _____ bread.

4. He's eating _____ cookies.

16. Questions with Quantifiers

On a piece of paper, write five or more statements about the picture of the restaurant on page 176. Use *many, a lot of, some, a few,* and *a little.*

Example There are some people in the restaurant.

Unit 5 Wrap-Up Activities

1. The Fourth of July: READING

Read this paragraph.

Today is July 4. It's Independence Day. It's an important holiday in the United States. Right now it's 4:00 in the afternoon. It's hot and sunny. My family is having a party. Many friends and relatives are here with us. There is a lot of food on a table in the backyard. I can see hamburgers and hot dogs on the table. There is salad, corn, bread, and watermelon. The watermelon is delicious. There are many things to drink, and there are a lot of great desserts: ice cream, cookies, strawberry shortcake, ... I like the Fourth of July.

strawberry shortcake

2. A Special Day: WRITING

Think about a holiday or another special day at home. Imagine you are there now. What day is it? What's the weather like? What are you eating? Write about it. Use expressions with *It's*, prepositions, count and noncount nouns, articles, and quantifiers.

3. Labor Day: EDITING

Correct the 12 errors. The first one is corrected for you.

Today is Labor Day. ~~Its~~ *It's* a holiday at the United States. It's in the first Monday in September. Me and my friends are going at the beach for the day. We're going in there car. I have a big picnic basket. Its full of good things to eat and drink: fruits, cookies, the sandwiches, a chips, many soda, and juice. The weather are great for a picnic on the beach!

4. Let's Find Out: SPEAKING/WRITING

Step One: Work with a partner to write six questions for your classmates. Use *How much* and *How many.*

1. phone calls/make in a day _____

2. e-mail messages/get in a day _____

3. soda/drink in a day _____

4. time/spend watching TV _____

5. _____

6. _____

Step Two: Find a new partner. Ask and answer your questions from Step One.

> **Example** *Student A:* How much time do you spend shopping on the weekend?
>
> *Student B:* A few hours.

Record your partner's answers. Then report two facts about him/her to the class.

1. _____   4. _____

2. _____   5. _____

3. _____   6. _____

5. Guess the Place: SPEAKING/LISTENING

Work in a group. One person thinks of a place and describes it. The other people listen and guess the place. Take turns.

> **Example** *Student A:* There are some tables and chairs in this place. There is a long desk, and there are a few people in back of the desk. There are many newspapers and books. . .
>
> *Students B and C:* It's the library!

GRAMMAR SUMMARY

It + the Time, Day, Date, or Weather

QUESTIONS	ANSWERS
What time is it?	**It's** five o'clock.
What's the weather like?	**It's** cool and cloudy.

★ See the Grammar Briefing on page 152.

Prepositions

PREPOSITIONS FOR DESCRIBING TIME

Class begins **at** 9:00. It lasts **from** 9:00 **to** 9:50. We have class **for** 50 minutes.

PREPOSITIONS FOR DESCRIBING LOCATION OR PLACE

The college is **on** Homestead Avenue **in** Holyoke, **near** the mall.

★ See the Grammar Briefings on pages 155 and 158.

Object Pronouns

She loves **me.**	They know **us.**
I love **you.**	They know **you.**
We love **him/her/it.**	We know **them.**

★ See the Grammar Briefing on page 161.

Count and Noncount Nouns; Articles *A/An* and *The*

COUNT NOUNS		NONCOUNT NOUNS
SINGULAR	PLURAL	
an apple	apples	fruit
a dollar	dollars	money

She's sitting under **a tree. The tree** is green. **The sun** is shining.

★ See the Grammar Briefings on pages 167 and 170.

Questions with *Is There* and *Are There*

WITH NONCOUNT/SINGULAR COUNT NOUNS	WITH PLURAL COUNT NOUNS

Is there | **time** for a movie? | **Are there movies** in the afternoon?

Is there | **a movie theater** at the mall?

★ See the Grammar Briefing on page 172.

Quantifiers; Questions with *How Many* and *How Much*

There is **some** delicious food on the table.

How many cookies do we have? **A lot.**

How much watermelon is there? Only **a little.**

★ See the Grammar Briefing on page 174.

TEST YOURSELF ON CHAPTER 9

1. Write statements with *It's* about the time, day, date, and weather.

    1. Wed. <u>It's Wednesday.</u>

    2. Sat. _____   5. _____

    3. 2:00 _____

    4. 11/21 _____   6. _____

2. Complete the sentences with the correct prepositions.

    1. I watch the news (a) <u>from</u> 6:00 (b) _____ 6:30. I watch it (c) _____ 30 minutes.

    2. It's hot here (a) _____ the summer. It starts getting cool (b) _____ September.

    3. I see my friends (a) _____ Saturdays. We have no classes (b) _____ weekends.

    4. They live (a) _____ New York. Their apartment is (b) _____ 1285 Fifth Ave.

    5. Lee works (a) _____ a bank. The bank is (b) _____ Main St. (c) _____ the post office and City Hall. Her office is (d) _____ the fourth floor.

3. Complete the sentences with object pronouns.

    1. Look at Mr. Hill. Do you see _____?

    2. Where's our beach umbrella? Can you see _____?

    3. We'd like to talk to you. Please call _____.

    4. She loves Jack, but he doesn't love _____.

    5. I don't know Yoko's parents. Do you know _____?

4. Find the six errors and correct them.

    1. I go to bed at 11:00 ~~in the~~ ^{at} night.

    2. Its a rainy day.

    3. Me and Chris like warm weather.

    4. Sang Youn usually sits back of Juan.

    5. The nurse's office is next the school library.

    6. Come here and sit near I.

TEST YOURSELF ON CHAPTER 10

5. Circle the correct word.

1. I'd like (an/—) ice in my soda, please.
2. They're buying (a/—) new furniture.
3. The food (look/looks) delicious.
4. The mail (is/are) on the table.
5. Would you like (a/—) sandwich?
6. She doesn't eat (a/—) cookies or candy.

6. Write *the* or – (no article).

1. They never eat _____ meat.
2. Do you take _____ sugar in your tea?
3. I like _____ coffee at that restaurant.
4. We buy _____ grapes in the summer.
5. _____ weather is wonderful today.
6. *A:* Where's _____ cat? *B:* He's outside.

7. Write questions with *be + there*. Add prepositions and the words in parentheses.

1. (nice beaches/your country) Are there nice beaches in your country?
2. (a lot of people/your class) _____
3. (a bus/8:30) _____
4. (good food/that restaurant) _____

8. Circle the correct quantifiers.

1. *A:* Do we need (any/many) bread from the store?

   B: No, we have (much/a lot of) bread, but we need (a little/a few) butter.

2. *A:* (How many/How much) fruit do you eat?

   B: (Not many/Not much), but I eat (a lot of/much) vegetables.

9. Find the six errors and correct them.

1. Would you like ˰ apple? *[an]*
2. People in China eat many rice.
3. I don't have a lot of moneys.
4. Is there a mail for me?
5. There are a little strawberries on the table.
6. He never drinks the coffee or tea.

See Answer Key pages ANS-5 and ANS-6.

Looking Back

Chapter 11

What a Weekend!

- Simple past of *be: was* and *were*
- Past time expressions
- Simple past tense:
  Regular and irregular verbs
  Affirmative statements

Chapter 12

Long Ago

- Simple past tense:
  Yes/No questions and short answers
  Negative statements
  Wh- questions and answers
- More irregular verbs

What a Weekend!

GRAMMAR IN ACTION

Reading and Listening

A. Listen and read.

Henry: Hi, Debbie! How **was** your weekend?

Debbie: Oh, the usual. I **cleaned** the house, **shopped,** and **cooked.** Yesterday we **played** some tennis. That's all. What about you? How was your weekend?

Henry: My weekend was like a bad dream.

Debbie: What?! What do you mean?

Henry: Well, Eva **went** to her parents' house for the weekend, because they were sick . . .

Debbie: So you **were** home alone with the kids?

Henry: Yup. And Friday evening, the baby **got** an ear infection, so I **took** her to the hospital.

Debbie: Poor thing!

Henry: We were there for HOURS. She **cried** all night, but she was fine the next day. Then Max was in a fight and **got** a black eye. . . .

Debbie: Oh, dear!

Henry: And yesterday, Joey **had** an accident with the car.

Debbie: I hope he's OK!

Henry: He's fine. He wasn't hurt—nobody was hurt—and it wasn't his fault. But I was pretty upset . . .

Debbie: I can imagine! Boy, what a weekend!

B. Work with a partner. Practice the conversation in Part A.

Think about Grammar

A. Complete these sentences from the conversation. Write the past forms of *be*.

1. *Henry:* Hi, Debbie! How _____ your weekend?

2. *Henry:* Well, Eva went to her parents' house for the weekend, because they

   _____ sick. . . .

3. *Debbie:* So you _____ home alone with the kids?

4. *Henry:* We _____ there for HOURS.

5. *Henry:* He's fine—he _____ hurt . . . .

6. *Henry:* But I _____ pretty upset. . . .

B. Write the **boldfaced** verbs from the conversation in the chart.

REGULAR VERBS		IRREGULAR VERBS	
BASE FORM	SIMPLE PAST FORM	BASE FORM	SIMPLE PAST FORM
1. clean	cleaned	1. be	was/were
2. shop	_____	2. go	_____
3. cook	_____	3. get	_____
4. play	_____	4. take	_____
5. cry	_____	5. have	_____

C. All **regular** simple past tense verbs end in the same two letters. What are they? _____

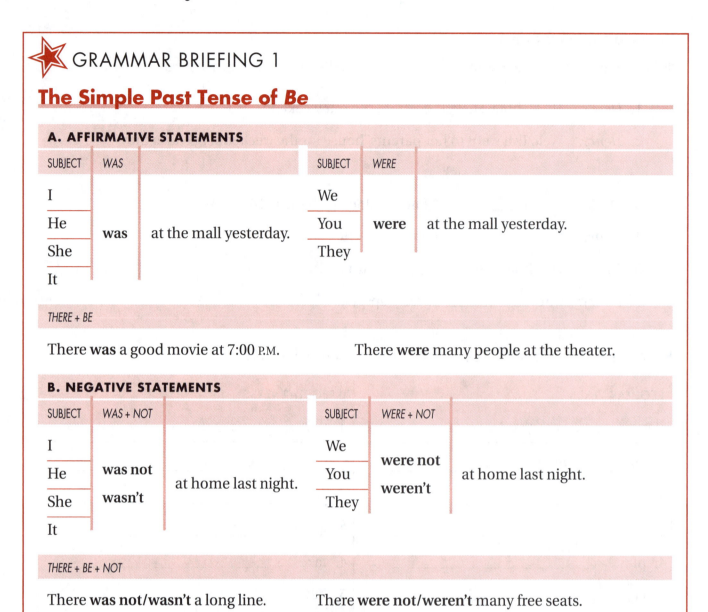

⭐ GRAMMAR BRIEFING 1

The Simple Past Tense of *Be*

A. AFFIRMATIVE STATEMENTS

SUBJECT	WAS		SUBJECT	WERE	
I He She It	**was**	at the mall yesterday.	We You They	**were**	at the mall yesterday.

THERE + BE

There **was** a good movie at 7:00 P.M.   There **were** many people at the theater.

B. NEGATIVE STATEMENTS

SUBJECT	WAS + NOT		SUBJECT	WERE + NOT	
I He She It	**was not** **wasn't**	at home last night.	We You They	**were not** **weren't**	at home last night.

THERE + BE + NOT

There **was not/wasn't** a long line.   There **were not/weren't** many free seats.

1. Simple Past Forms of *Be*

Write *was* or *were*. Use contractions in negative statements.

1. *Grace:* The driving ___was___ terrible Friday night. It _____ so foggy!

                    a   b

   Ed: Yeah, there _____ two accidents on Rt. 15.

                          c

   Grace: Did you see them?

   Ed: One of them. We _____ on our way to a movie.

                                d

2. *Luis:* Hey, you (+ *not*) _____ at the game on Saturday!

                                  a

   Ray: Yeah, I _____ sick.

                       b

3. *Sue:* John _____ at the party Saturday night, but Anna (+ *not*)
         a

_____ with him.
   b

   Pam: I know. She _____ with me. We _____ at the mall.
                             c   d

2. Simple Past Forms of *Be*

Write *was* or *were*. Use contractions in negative statements.

Today in the United States, "the weekend" means Saturday and Sunday. Most people

don't work on these two days. They have free time. This (+ *not*) __*wasn't*__ always
                                                                 1

true. Before 1938, factory workers usually (+ *not*) _____ free on Saturday. They
                                                            2

_____ at work. Their work week _____ long: 60 hours, 70 hours, ... It
   3   4

(+ *not*) _____ good for the workers. Then in 1938, there _____ a new
           5   6

law in the United States. It _____ a big help to workers. This _____ the
                         7   8

beginning of the two-day weekend.

a **law** = a rule made by the government of a country or a state.

 ☀ **Grammar Hotspot!**

Was and *were* are often used with **past time expressions.** A past time expression tells when something happened.

> Today is Monday. **Yesterday was** Sunday.
>
> He **was** at home **yesterday morning/ afternoon/evening.**
>
> We **were** out **last night.**
>
> He **wasn't** here **last week/last month/ last year.**
>
> We **were** there an hour/two days/a few years **ago.**

3. Past Time Expressions

Write *last*, *ago*, or *yesterday*.

1. I was here ___last___ year.

2. We weren't in school a month _____.

3. Were you at home _____ morning?

4. I was in bed at 11:00 _____ night.

5. He was here five minutes _____!

6. There was no homework _____.

7. _____ week was school vacation.

8. Were you a student a year _____?

9. I was late _____ morning.

10. It was hot the day before _____.

4. Making Statements with *Was* and *Were*

Work in a group. Each person takes three pieces of paper. Don't show your papers to the group. Write: (1) the name(s) of one or two classmates, (2) a place (for example, *on the moon, in Hollywood*), and (3) one or two famous people. Put all the papers face down in three separate piles. Each person takes one paper from each pile and tells this story:

> Last night, I had a strange dream. _____ (was/were) in my dream
>   classmate(s)
>
> with me. We were _____. _____ (was/were) with us, too.
>   a place   famous person(s)

Take turns. You can add more to the story.

Example *Student A:* Last night, I had a strange dream. Yoko and Yusef, you were in my dream with me. We were on a big boat on the ocean. Superman was with us, too. There was a big storm. It was a bad dream!

GRAMMAR BRIEFING 2
Questions with *Was/Were*

A. *YES/NO* QUESTIONS AND SHORT ANSWERS

QUESTIONS			ANSWERS		
WAS/WERE	SUBJECT		YES		NO
	I			I **was.**	I **wasn't.**
	he			he **was.**	he **wasn't.**
Was	she			she **was.**	she **wasn't.**
	it	late?	Yes,	it **was.**	No, it **wasn't.**
	we			we **were.**	we **weren't.**
Were	you			you **were.**	you **weren't.**
	they			they **were.**	they **weren't.**

B. *WH-* QUESTIONS AND ANSWERS

QUESTIONS			ANSWERS
WH- QUESTION WORD	WAS/WERE		
Where	**were**	you last night?	At a party.
Who	**was**	at the party?	A lot of people from our building.
How	**was**	it?	Great!

Talking the Talk

Use *How was/were* to ask for a description or an opinion of something.

Q: **How was** your weekend?
A: It was terrific!

Q: **How were** your final exams?
A: Hard.

5. Questions and Answers with *Was/Were*

A. Read the questions and answers in Part B.

Tickets

B. Listen to the conversation between two students, Steve and Josh. Circle the answers.

1. Where was Josh on Saturday night? a. At a sports event. b. At a concert.

2. Where was it? a. At Ward College. b. At Ward Stadium.

3. Was it fun? a. Yes, it was great. b. No, not really.

4. Who was there? a. A few people. b. A lot of people.

5. How much were tickets? a. $10 or more. b. $100 or more.

6. Yes/No Questions and Short Answers

Rewrite each statement as a *yes/no* question. Write the short answers.

1. I wasn't home last night.

   Were you home last night? No, I wasn't.
   _____

2. We were at the mall.

   _____

3. You weren't late.

   _____

4. He was in class this morning.

   _____

5. They were at a party Saturday night.

   _____

6. She wasn't at the concert.

   _____

7. It was fun.

   _____

7. *Wh- Questions with Was/Were*

A. Complete the conversations. Use *Where, How, Who, Why,* or *When + was/were*.

1. *A:* _Where were_____ you last night?
      _a

   B: I was at a movie.

   A: _____ it?
          _b

   B: It was really funny!

2. *A:* _____ you this morning?
          _a

   You weren't in class.

   B: I was at a job interview.

   A: _____ it?
          _b

   B: At the University Bookstore.

   A: _____ the interview?
          _c

   B: It was great! I have a new job now.

3. *A:* _____ you and Bob
          _a

   Saturday last night?

   B: We were at a party.

   A: _____ there?
          _b

   B: Friends of Bob's from college.

4. *A:* I was in Québec last year.

   B: Really? _____ you there?
                  _a

   A: In the spring—in April.

   B: _____ you there?
          _b

   A: Because I was on vacation.

B. Work with a partner. Read the conversations in Part A.

8. Questions with *Was/Were*

Work in a group. Student A: Make a statement about a place you were in the past. Other students: Ask *wh-* and *yes/no* questions. Take turns.

Example   *Student A:* I was in Florida last year.

   Student B: Were you at Disney World?

   Student A: No, I was in school in Miami.

   Student C: How was it? Was it a good school?

GRAMMAR BRIEFING 3

The Simple Past of Regular Verbs

A. AFFIRMATIVE STATEMENTS IN THE SIMPLE PAST

SUBJECT	BASE VERB + -(E)D	
I		
We		
You		
They	**started**	in 1995.
He		
She		
It		

B. SPELLING RULES*

Add -*(e)d* to the base form of a regular verb for the simple past tense form.

1. Most verbs: Add -*ed.*

   watch ➔ watch**ed**   play ➔ play**ed**

2. Verbs that end in *e:* Add -*d.*

   smile ➔ smil**ed**   dance ➔ danc**ed**

3. Verbs that end in a consonant† + *y:*
   Drop the *y* and add -*ied.*

   stu**dy** ➔ stud**ied**   try ➔ tr**ied**

*See Appendix 7 for more spelling rules.
†See page 2 for lists of the consonants and vowels.

Grammar Hotspot!

For most verbs that end in "C V C"
   (consonant + vowel + consonant):
   Double the final consonant and add -*ed.*

   stop ➔ stop**ped**

   control ➔ control**led**

9. Simple Past Tense of Regular Verbs

A. Read about Joe's weekends.

My weekends are always the same. On Friday night, I party with my friends. Saturday morning, I stay in bed pretty late. Then I pick up my apartment. In the afternoon, I shop for groceries, and I wash clothes at the laundromat. Then it's time to relax! I usually play video games with friends. Sometimes we watch sports on TV. On Sunday, I work out at the gym. Then I study at the library for the rest of the day. In the evening, I call my parents.

B. Last weekend was the same as usual for Joe. Complete the statements. Use the simple past tense.

1. On Friday night, Joe _partied with his friends._____

2. On Saturday morning, he _____

3. Then _____

4. He needed food, so _____

5. At the laundromat, _____

6. As usual, _____

7. They also _____ a basketball game on TV.

8. On Sunday morning, _____

9. For the rest of the day, _____

10. In the evening, _____

10. Simple Past Tense of Regular Verbs

Student A: Ask *Do you ever . . . ?* questions with the words in the box. Student B: You can answer *No, I never do.* or *Yes,* + the last time you did it. Take turns.

Example *Student A:* Do you ever play sports?
  Student B: Yes, I played volleyball last week.

ask questions in class	play cards	study outside
call your parents	play sports	use a dictionary
cook	remember your dreams	watch the news on TV
cry	rent videos/DVDs	work out at a gym

Talking the Talk

1. Sometimes the *-ed* ending adds a syllable. This happens when the base verb ends in the sound /t/ or /d/.

• hate	• • hated
• need	• • needed
• • expect	• • • expected

2. Sometimes the *-ed* ending on a verb doesn't sound like /d/. It sounds like /t/.

talked, watched, kissed, washed, laughed, stopped, fixed

See Appendix 7 for more information.

11. Pronunciation of –*ed* Verb Endings

A. Listen to the sentences. Does the verb ending sound like /d/ or /t/?

1. Joe **partied** on Friday night. (/d/) /t/
2. He **stayed** in bed late. /d/ /t/
3. He **cleaned** up the apartment. /d/ /t/
4. He **shopped** at Dino's Market. /d/ /t/
5. He **washed** a lot of clothes. /d/ /t/
6. He **played** a video game. /d/ /t/
7. He **watched** a game on TV. /d/ /t/
8. He **worked** out. /d/ /t/
9. He **studied** at the library. /d/ /t/
10. He **called** his parents. /d/ /t/

B. Work with a partner. Say each statement. Does the *-(e)d* add a syllable? Circle *Yes* or *No*.

1. I **learned** about the concert from an ad on the radio. Yes (No)
2. I **waited** in line for the show. Yes No
3. I **needed** to buy a ticket. Yes No
4. I **wanted** to see the singer. Yes No
5. I **expected** to enjoy the concert. Yes No
6. I **enjoyed** it very much. Yes No

C. Listen to the verbs from Part B. Check your answers.

GRAMMAR BRIEFING 4

The Simple Past of Irregular Verbs

Irregular verbs do not add *-ed* in the simple past tense. They have different forms:

BASE FORM	SIMPLE PAST TENSE FORM	BASE FORM	SIMPLE PAST TENSE FORM	BASE FORM	SIMPLE PAST TENSE FORM
buy	**bought**	get	**got**	make	**made**
do	**did**	go	**went**	see	**saw**
eat	**ate**	have	**had**	take	**took**

12. Verb Forms

A. Write the simple past tense form of the verb.

1. go ___went___
2. have _____
3. do _____

4. make _____
5. see _____
6. buy _____

7. eat _____
8. take _____
9. get _____

B. Student A: Say a statement from the list below. Add a time expression with *every*. Student B: Close your book and listen. Change the statement to the past. Add *yesterday*.

Example   *Student A:* I *do my homework every night.*
               Student B: I *did my homework yesterday.*

1. I do my homework.
2. I see her at school.
3. They have lunch at 1:00.

4. John buys coffee.
5. Ann takes the bus.
6. Mike goes fishing.

7. The boys get hungry.
8. We make some mistakes.
9. I eat a good breakfast.

C. Change roles: now Student B begins.

1. Mr. Han buys flowers.
2. Lisa takes pictures.
3. They go dancing.

4. I do the dishes.
5. The children get tired.
6. We make some mistakes.

7. She eats a lot of fruit.
8. Nora has lunch at 1:00.
9. You see me at school.

13. Simple Past of Irregular Verbs

A. Read about the Herreras.

On Saturdays, Mr. and Mrs. Herrera take care of their grandson. They usually:

go to the park	take food for the birds	buy ice cream at the snack bar
see old friends	take pictures	get a drink at the water fountain
make new friends	eat at a picnic table	have a lot of fun

B. Work with a partner. Look at the pictures. They show what the Herreras did last Saturday. Tell the story. Give as much information as you can.

> Example   *Student A:* On Saturday, Mr. and Mrs. Herrera went to the park.
>
> *Student B:* They went by car. The name of the park was Oak Park.

C. What did you do last Saturday? Write a paragraph about your day.

EXTRA PRACTICE

14. Past Tense of *Be*

Write *was* or *were*. Use contractions in negative statements.

Subj: Hi
From: gee_washburn@southstate.edu
To: Kate_Hollis@southstate.edu

Hi Katie! I _____ at the Stompers concert last night. Your brother Josh
⠀⠀⠀⠀⠀⠀⠀⠀⠀1

_____ there, too. He (not) _____ with anyone. He said you (not)
⠀⠀2⠀⠀⠀⠀⠀⠀⠀⠀⠀⠀⠀⠀⠀⠀⠀⠀⠀3

_____ there because you _____ sick. I hope you're feeling better today.
⠀⠀4⠀⠀⠀⠀⠀⠀⠀⠀⠀⠀⠀⠀⠀⠀⠀⠀5

The band _____ cool. Our seats _____ great—we _____ in
⠀⠀⠀⠀⠀⠀⠀⠀6⠀⠀⠀⠀⠀⠀⠀⠀⠀⠀⠀⠀⠀⠀7⠀⠀⠀⠀⠀⠀⠀⠀⠀⠀⠀⠀8

Row 3! The stadium (not) _____ full. There _____ a lot of empty seats.
⠀⠀⠀⠀⠀⠀⠀⠀⠀⠀⠀⠀⠀⠀9⠀⠀⠀⠀⠀⠀⠀⠀⠀⠀⠀⠀10

Love, Gee

---

15. Questions with *Was/Were*

A. Write *yes/no* questions with *was/were*. Write the short answers.

1. you/at the movies last night (yes) _Were you at the movies last night? Yes, I was._____

2. the weather/nice last week (yes) _____

3. the stores/open yesterday (no) _____

4. Steve/at the concert (no) _____

5. you/here last year (no) _____

6. the people/friendly (yes) _____

7. I/late (no) _____

8. we/in Room 100 (yes) _____

9. the test/hard (no) _____

10. your sister/in the same class (yes) _____

B. Rewrite each statement as a *wh-* question. Write the **boldfaced** words as the answers.

1. They were **in the park.** _Where were they? In the park._

2. **My sister** was on the phone. _____

3. I was **at a party** last night. _____

4. The movie was **great.** _____

5. My exams were **easy.** _____

6. They were **in New York.** _____

7. **My brother** was with me. _____

8. The man's name was **Robert.** _____

16. Regular Verbs in the Simple Past

Change each statement to the past. Add a time expression.

1. He plays video games. _He played video games last weekend._

2. She smiles at me. _____

3. We try some new foods. _____

4. They stop at all red lights. _____

5. I pick up my room. _____

6. We work out at the gym. _____

7. Al and his wife shop at the mall. _____

8. The students listen. _____

9. The baby cries all night. _____

10. My friends rent videos. _____

17. Irregular Verbs in the Simple Past

Write nine true statements in the simple past tense. Use all the verbs in the list below.

buy, do, eat, get, go, have, make, see, take

GRAMMAR IN ACTION

Reading and Listening

A. Listen and read.

Henry: So, Daniel, you're from Taiwan, aren't you?

Daniel: Yes, that's right. I was born in Taipei.

Henry: Where did you grow up?

Daniel: In Taipei. My parents still live there.

Henry: And when did you come to the U.S.?

Daniel: I **came** about a year ago. I wanted to work in international business, but I didn't speak much English.

Henry: Did you start to learn English just last year?!

Daniel: Oh, no! I started in third grade. But for a long time, I didn't take it seriously. At the university, I **began** to think about my future. Then I **met** my wife and decided to come here to study.

Henry: Did she come with you?

Daniel: Oh, of course! And our baby, too.

was born = started life. **grow up** = live from being a young child to being an adult.
take (something) seriously = think that (something) is important.

B. Work with a partner. Practice the conversation in Part A.

Think about Grammar

A. Look at the three **boldfaced** words in the conversation. They are irregular verbs. Write them in the chart. Then write the base form of each verb.

BASE FORM	SIMPLE PAST TENSE FORM
_____	_____
_____	_____
_____	_____

B. Complete these sentences from the conversation. Circle the main verb.

1. *Henry:* And __when did you (come)__ to the U.S.?

2. *Daniel:* . . . , but I _____ much English.

3. *Henry:* _____ to learn English just last year?!

4. *Daniel:* But for a long time, _____ it seriously.

5. *Henry:* _____ with you?

Look at the negative statements. What form is the main verb? Circle your answer:

      base form   simple past tense form

Look at the *yes/no* and *wh-* questions. What form is the main verb?

      base form   simple past tense form

C. Work with a partner. Ask these questions. Write your partner's answers. Tell the class about your partner.

1. When did you start to learn English? _____

2. Where did you start to learn English? _____

3. Why did you study English then? _____

4. Why are you studying English now? _____

GRAMMAR BRIEFING 1

Yes/No Questions in the Simple Past

YES/NO QUESTIONS			SHORT ANSWERS			
DID	SUBJECT	BASE VERB	YES		NO	
Did	I we you they he she it	**win?**	Yes,	I we you they he she it	**did.**	No,	I we you they he she it	**did not.** **didn't.**

REGULAR AND IRREGULAR VERBS

Form simple past *yes/no* questions the same way for both regular and irregular verbs.

Regular verb: **Did** you **like** the movie?

Irregular verb: **Did** you **have** fun?

See Chapter 11, Grammar Briefing 2, page 191, for *yes/no* questions with *was/were*.

1. Yes/No Questions and Short Answers

Complete the questions with the words in parentheses. Write the short answers.

1. *A:* (you/have) __Did you have__ fun?

   B: Yes, __I did__ . It was a great party.

2. *A:* (we/miss) _____ the bus?

   B: No, _____ . Here it comes!

3. *A:* (I/make) _____ any mistakes?

   B: No, _____ . You did a great job.

4. *A:* (Bill/like) _____ the movie?

   B: No, _____ . He hated it.

5. *A:* (you/do) _____ the homework?

   B: Yes, _____ . It was easy.

6. *A:* (Maria/call) _____ ?

   B: Yes, _____ , but she'll call back.

7. *A:* (their team/win) _____ ?

   B: Yes, _____ They won 2 to 1.

8. *A:* (you/have) _____ a test?

   B: No, _____ .

Talking the Talk

People sometimes pronounce *did you* as "didja" or "ja."

WRITE	YOU WILL OFTEN HEAR
Did you have fun?	"Didja" have fun? "Ja" have fun?

2. Asking and Answering Questions with *Did you . . . ?*

A. Student A: Close your book. Listen and answer the questions. Student B: Ask your partner about his or her childhood. Check (✓) your partner's answers, and take notes under "More Information." Take turns asking the questions.

Example   *Student B:* When you were a child, did you have a pet?

Student A: Yes, I did. I had a cat. Her name was Itza, and she was black.

OR No, I didn't. My mother didn't like animals.

When you were a child . . .	Yes	No	More information?
have a pet			
live in a big city			
play sports			
take music lessons			
travel with your family			
other: _____			
_____			

B. Take turns telling the class something about your partner. Ask your classmates more questions.

Example   *Student B:* Yoko didn't have a pet. Her mother didn't like animals.

Student C: Did you want a pet?

Student A: Yes, I wanted a cat.

GRAMMAR BRIEFING 2

Negative Statements in the Simple Past

SUBJECT	DID + NOT	BASE VERB
I		
We		
You	**did not**	**win.**
They	**didn't**	
He		
She		
It		

REGULAR AND IRREGULAR VERBS

Form simple past negative statements the same way for both regular and irregular verbs.

Regular verb: **I didn't like** the movie.

Irregular verb: **I didn't have** fun.

See Chapter 11, Grammar Briefing 1, page 188, for negative statements with *was/were*.

3. Negative Statements, Simple Past Tense

A. All these statements about the story of Little Red Riding Hood are false. Rewrite them as negative statements.

Little Red Riding Hood and the wolf

1. Little Red Riding Hood wanted to visit a friend. _She didn't want to visit a friend._

2. Her mother went with her. _____

3. She took a basket of money. _____

4. She talked with a wolf at a bus stop. _____

5. The wolf took the long way through the woods. _____

6. The girl got to her grandmother's house first. _____

7. She called for help on her cell phone. _____

8. The wolf ate Little Red Riding Hood. _____

B. Work in a group. Read your statements. Who can tell the real story of Little Red Riding Hood?

4. Affirmative and Negative Statements, Simple Past Tense

A. Work with a partner. Talk about your life at school when you were a child. Tell if you did or didn't do the things on the list.

Example   *Student A:* 1. I didn't start school at age five. I was six years old.
                         I went to a girls' school near my home.

1. start school at age five

2. have a school uniform

3. take a bus to school

4. like my teachers

5. learn English in school

6. eat lunch at school

7. like to read

8. have a lot of homework

These girls are wearing their school uniform.

GRAMMAR BRIEFING 3

More Irregular Verbs

BASE FORM	SIMPLE PAST TENSE FORM	BASE FORM	SIMPLE PAST TENSE FORM	BASE FORM	SIMPLE PAST TENSE FORM
begin	**began**	drink	**drank**	read	**read**
bring	**brought**	leave	**left**	run	**ran**
come	**came**	meet	**met**	sleep	**slept**

5. Verb Forms

A. Write the simple past tense form of the verb.

1. read _____read_____

2. come _____

3. leave _____

4. begin _____

5. run _____

6. meet _____

7. sleep _____

8. drink _____

9. bring _____

B. Student A: Say a statement from the list below. Add a time expression with *every*. Student B: Close your book. Listen. Change the statement to the past. Add a past time expression.

Example   *Student A:* She drinks tea every morning.

   Student B: She drank tea yesterday morning.

1. The movie begins at 8:00.
2. We meet new people.
3. They come to class late.
4. I sleep like a baby.
5. She reads the newspaper.
6. He runs two miles.
7. The bus leaves at 3:00.
8. I bring my books to class.
9. They drink coffee.

C. Change roles with your partner. Now Student B begins.

1. The plane leaves at 4:00.
2. She meets her friends.
3. You come on time.
4. The game begins at 2:00.
5. We bring our books.
6. They drink tea.
7. She sleeps for eight hours.
8. He reads his mail.
9. They run a mile.

6. Simple Past Tense Statements, Irregular Verbs

A. Work in a group. Did you hear the story of Snow White when you were a child? These pictures tell part of her story. Number them in order. Use them to tell this part of the story. Add information when you can.

____meet the Seven Dwarfs

____ come to a little house

1   leave home

____run into the forest

____begin cleaning

____sleep on a little bed

B. Listen to the whole story of Snow White.

C. Tell the last part of the story. Here is some important vocabulary:

Snow White's stepmother

the poisoned apple

the handsome prince

GRAMMAR BRIEFING 4

Wh- Questions in the Simple Past

WH- QUESTION WORD	DID	SUBJECT	BASE VERB		ANSWERS
Where		I	**leave**	my keys?	On the table.
Who/Whom*		you	**see?**		Mr. and Mrs. Yilmaz.
When	**did**	she	**call**	you?	Yesterday.
What		they	**want?**		Some information.
Why		it	**happen?**		I don't know.

Whom is used in formal English.

REGULAR AND IRREGULAR VERBS

Form simple past *wh-* questions the same way for both regular and irregular verbs.

See Chapter 11, Grammar Briefing 2, page 191, for *wh-* questions with *was/were.*

Regular verb: When **did** he **call?**

Irregular verb: When **did** he **leave?**

7. *Wh-* Questions and Answers

Match the questions and answers about the story of Snow White (page 208).

_b_ 1. Why did Snow White leave home?

____ 2. Where did she go?

____ 3. What did she do in the little house?

____ 4. What did she eat?

____ 5. How long did she sleep?

____ 6. What did the prince do?

____ 7. How did the story end?

a. She began to clean it.

b. Because her stepmother was mean and cruel.

c. He kissed her, and she woke up.

d. Snow White married the prince.

e. For many years.

f. Into the forest.

g. A poisoned apple.

8. *Wh-* Questions and Answers

A. Write *wh-* questions about the **boldfaced** words.

My Life

by Daniel Chun

I was born in Taiwan in 1981. I grew up (1) **in the city of Taipei.**
(2) **I started school** in 1986. I began learning English (3) **in the third grade.**
(4) **After I finished high school,** I went to university. I studied (5) **business.**
I got married (6) **when I was 21.**

QUESTIONS	ANSWERS
1. Where did Daniel grow up?	In Taipei.
2. _____	He started school.
3. _____	In the third grade.
4. _____	After he finished high school.
5. _____	Business.
6. _____	When he was 21.

B. Write six questions to ask a classmate about his or her life. Include four or more *wh-* questions in the simple past tense.

Example Where did you grow up?

1. _____
2. _____
3. _____
4. _____
5. _____
6. _____

C. Work with a partner. Ask your questions. Then tell the class about your partner.

EXTRA PRACTICE

9. *Yes/No Questions in the Simple Past, Regular and Irregular Verbs*

Complete the conversations with *yes/no* questions and short answers. Use the **boldfaced** verbs in your questions.

1. *A:* ___Did you have_____ a good time?

   B: Yes, we _____ . We **had** a WONDERFUL time!

2. *A:* _____ a new car?

   B: No, they _____ . They **bought** a used car.

3. *A:* _____ down Green Street?

   B: No, it _____ . The bus **went** down Market Street.

4. *A:* _____ a good grade on the test?

   B: Yes, she _____ . She **got** 95%.

5. *A:* _____ last night?

   B: No, _____ . But it's **raining** now.

6. *A:* _____ the game?

   B: Yes, _____ . They **won** 2 to 1.

7. *A:* _____ at 12:00?

   B: Yes, _____ . I **ate** with Luis.

8. *A:* _____ all the cookies?

   B: Yes, _____ . We **finished** all the milk, too.

10. Statements in the Simple Past, Regular and Irregular Verbs

Write about your life when you were a child. Write eight or more true affirmative and negative statements. Use regular and irregular verbs.

Example   I started school at age four.

I didn't have a pet.

11. Irregular Verbs in the Simple Past Tense

A. Write the simple past tense form.

1. sleep   _____

2. run   _____

3. read   _____

4. meet   _____

5. leave   _____

6. drink   _____

7. come   _____

8. bring   _____

9. begin   _____

B. Write true statements about your past life. Use all the irregular verbs in Part A.

Examples   I met my girlfriend six months ago.

My brother came to visit me last week.

12. *Wh-* Questions in the Simple Past Tense

Write *wh-* questions to ask for the missing information.

1. They had their party last . . . _When did they have their party?_____

2. I grew up in . . . _____

3. She married him in 19— _____

4. They bought a . . . _____

5. He called her because . . . _____

6. I met . . . yesterday. _____

7. He read . . . to the class. _____

8. I . . . last weekend. _____

9. I bought them at . . . _____

10. They finished at . . . o'clock. _____

Unit 6 Wrap-Up Activities

1. Henry's Life: READING

Read this paragraph.

Henry O'Leary teaches psychology at Springfield Community College. He was born in Texas in 1960, and he grew up in California and Ohio. He grew up with a brother and two sisters. They went to public schools. In high school, Henry was a good baseball player. After high school, he went to Ohio State University. He met his wife there. Her name is Eva. They got married in 1985. Now they have three children. Henry began teaching in 1986. He likes his job. He also likes reading, fishing, and going to Mexican restaurants.

2. Your Life: WRITING

Write about your life. Answer these questions: Where were you born? Where did you grow up? Where did you go to school? What did you like to do when you were a child? What do you like to do now? Use regular and irregular past tense verbs.

3. Beatriz: EDITING

Correct the ten verb errors. The first error is corrected for you.

My name is Beatriz Espada. I was born in Mexico, and
I ~~was grow up~~ *grew up* in Mexico. I was lived with my parents
and my three brothers. I didn't had any sisters. Our house
were small but very nice. We were go to a private school
near my home. I had many friends there, and I plaied
with them after school. On vacations, I like to visit my
grandparents in the country. They're had a farm, and
there was many animals. After high school, I comed here
and now I live in the city. I miss the country.

4. Find Someone Who: SPEAKING/LISTENING

Step One: Look at statements 1–8. With a partner, practice asking the questions with *Were you* and *Did you*.

Step Two: Walk around the room. Ask your classmates the questions. Write different names on the lines. Make true statements.

> Example   *Student A:* Mao, did you go shopping this past weekend?
>
> *Student B:* No, I didn't.
>
> *Student A* can write: ___Mao___ didn't go shopping this past weekend.

1. _____ was in bed at 10:30 last night.

2. _____ made a long-distance phone call yesterday.

3. _____ wasn't here one year ago.

4. _____ didn't go shopping this past weekend.

5. _____ saw a good movie not long ago.

6. _____ got a letter or some e-mail yesterday.

7. _____ was in a car accident.

8. _____ had fun last weekend.

5. Guess the Movie: SPEAKING/LISTENING

Work in a group. Student A: Think of a movie you saw. Start to tell what happened in the movie. Use the simple past tense. The others in the group try to guess the name of the movie.

> Example   *Student A:* I saw this movie a long time ago. It was a love story, and it was very sad. There were many people on a big ship. . . .
>
> *Group:* Titanic!

GRAMMAR SUMMARY

Past Time Expressions

I was here **yesterday.**

He called me **two days ago.**

They bought it **last week.**

★ See the Grammar Hotspot on page 189.

Simple Past Tense of *Be*

STATEMENTS

I/He/She/It	was	in New York.	We/You/They	were	in New York.
I/He/She/It	was not / wasn't	here.	We/You/They	were not / weren't	here.

QUESTIONS AND ANSWERS

Was	I/he/she/it	late?	Yes, I/he/she/it **was.**	No, I/he/she/it **wasn't.**
Were	we/you/they		Yes, we/you/they **were.**	No, we/you/they **weren't.**

Where were you?	At a movie.
How was it?	Very good.

★ See the Grammar Briefings on pages 188 and 191.

Simple Past Tense of Other Verbs

STATEMENTS

REGULAR VERBS	IRREGULAR VERBS
I **liked** the movie.	He **went** to a basketball game.
She **didn't like** it.	We **didn't go** with him.

QUESTIONS AND ANSWERS

Did it **rain**?	Yes, it **did.**/No, it **didn't.**
Did you **have** a good weekend?	Yes, I **did.**/No, I **didn't.**
What did you **watch**?	An old movie.
When did it **begin**?	At 9:00.

★ See the Grammar Briefings on pages 194, 197, 203, 205, and 207.

Spelling Rules for Regular Verbs in the Simple Past Tense

wash ➜ wash**ed**   dance ➜ danc**ed**

cry ➜ **cried**   stop ➜ stop**ped**

★ See the Grammar Briefing on page 194.

TEST YOURSELF ON CHAPTER 11

1. Complete the time expressions. Write *ago, last,* or *yesterday.*

   1. I got hungry about an hour _____ .
   2. Who did the dishes _____ night?
   3. It rained _____ afternoon.
   4. He got a haircut _____ .
   5. We lived there two years _____ .
   6. I went shopping _____ weekend.

2. Write the correct past tense form of *be.* Write contractions in negative statements.

   1. Bob _____ in school in 1995.
   2. (not) You _____ here then.
   3. There _____ two accidents.
   4. (not) It _____ windy.
   5. We _____ on vacation.
   6. Ann and I _____ in her room.

3. Put the words in order. Write the questions. Match them with their answers.

   1. was/he/when/in Boston   When was he in Boston? _____   ____ a. No, he was absent.
   2. you/where/were/at 2:00   _____   ____ b. Because he was sick.
   3. was/how/the weather   _____   _1_ c. Last summer.
   4. here on Monday/he/was   _____   ____ d. In my math class.
   5. absent/why/he/was   _____   ____ e. Great!

4. Complete the statements. Write the simple past tense of the verb in parentheses.

   1. (talk) He _talked_ to his friend.
   2. (buy) She _____ a guitar.
   3. (carry) He _____ her bags.
   4. (see) We _____ that movie.
   5. (watch) We _____ the news.
   6. (take) I _____ the bus.
   7. (hug) They _____ their friends.
   8. (eat) You _____ all the cookies!

5. Find the six errors and correct them.

   1. My feet ~~was~~ *were* cold.
   2. He was go to work by bus.
   3. You was right, and I was wrong.
   4. She made all her homework.
   5. The police stoped the driver.
   6. When you were at the mall?

TEST YOURSELF ON CHAPTER 12

6. Write *yes/no* questions and short answers.

    1. you/bring any money (no)   *Did you bring any money? No, I didn't.* _____

    2. the movie/end at 11:00 (yes) _____

    3. they/leave the room (yes) _____

    4. it/arrive on time (no) _____

    5. you/meet his new girlfriend (yes) _____

7. Rewrite the statements. Make them negative.

    1. The men robbed a bank. _____

    2. I slept very well. _____

    3. He tried the door. _____

8. Rewrite the sentences in the simple past tense.

    1. He runs to the gym. _____

    2. Do you read the newspaper? _____

    3. Her dog comes with her. _____

    4. Does he drink much soda? _____

9. Write *wh-* questions. The **boldfaced** words are the answers.

    1. The movie began **at 7:00.** _____

    2. I called **my brother.** _____

    3. They went **to San Francisco.** _____

    4. She ate **fruit salad.** _____

10. Find the six errors and correct them.

               didn't

    1. My brother ~~wasn't~~ have a car.   4. Did they all the homework?

    2. Where you went after work?   5. Janez and I weren't drink any coffee.

    3. I didn't bought much at the store.   6. Was he take his medicine?

See Answer Key pages ANS-6 and ANS-7.

Let's Look Ahead

Chapter 13

Looking Forward to the Future

- Expressing the future with *be going to:*
  Affirmative and negative statements
  Yes/No questions and short answers
  Wh- questions and answers
- Future time expressions

Chapter 14

Plans and Predictions

- Expressing the future with *will:*
  Affirmative and negative statements
  Yes/No questions and short answers
  Wh- questions and answers
- *Will* vs. *be going to*
- *Have to*

13 Looking Forward to the Future

GRAMMAR IN ACTION

Reading and Listening

A. Listen and read.

Mrs. Scott: My daughter's going to come home from college next week.

Nestor: Great! I bet you're looking forward to seeing her. What's she studying these days?

Mrs. Scott: She's taking a lot of science courses—chemistry, physics, ...

Nestor: Is she going to be a scientist? or a doctor?

Mrs. Scott: No, she's not. My son Johnny is going to be a doctor, but Janelle has other ideas.

Nestor: What is she going to do?

Mrs. Scott: In a few years, she's going to be an astronaut.

Nestor: Really?! Wow. . . . Why is she going to do that?

Mrs. Scott: Well, Janelle says, in the future, space is going to be very important. More and more people are probably going to travel there. And she wants to be one of them!

Nestor: Is she going to walk on the moon?

Mrs. Scott: It's possible . . . who knows?! Maybe we're all going to go there.

Nestor: No way! Not me!

look forward to = think of (something in the future) and feel happy. (*I'm looking forward to my vacation.*)

B. Work with a partner. Practice the conversation in Part A.

Think about Grammar

A. Look at these sentences from the conversation. Are the speakers talking about the present or the future? Check (✓) your answers.

	NOW	IN THE FUTURE
1. My daughter's going to come home from college.		✓
2. What's she studying these days?		
3. My son Johnny is going to be a doctor.		
4. Janelle has other ideas.		
5. Maybe we're all going to go there.		

Circle a or b:

The sentences about (a. the present/b. the future) all have *is/are going to*.

B. Complete the questions from the conversation.

YES/NO QUESTIONS	WH- QUESTIONS
1. <u>Is she going to be</u> a scientist?	3. What _____?
2. _____ on the moon?	4. Why _____ that?

C. What do these sentences from the conversation mean? Choose a or b.

1. "It's possible . . . who knows?!"
   a. Yes, it's going to happen. Who knows about it?
   b. Maybe yes, maybe no . . . nobody knows for sure.

2. "No way!"
   a. It's not going to happen. It's not possible.
   b. I don't think so, but I'm not sure.

D. Work in a group. Find out the answers to these questions:

1. How many people in the group would like to be astronauts? _____

2. How many people would like to visit the moon? _____

3. How many think there are going to be "Moon Vacations" in the future? _____

221

GRAMMAR BRIEFING 1

Expressing the Future with *Be Going To*

A. AFFIRMATIVE AND NEGATIVE STATEMENTS

SUBJECT	BE (+ NOT)	GOING TO	BASE VERB	
I	**am (not)**			
We				
You	**are (not)**			
They		**going to**	**leave**	tomorrow.
He				
She	**is (not)**			
It				

B. USING CONTRACTIONS

1. Use contractions with *be* in speaking and in informal writing.

> **I'm** going to leave soon. **I'm** not going to stay here.

2. Remember! There are two ways to form contractions with *are/is* + *not*.

> He **isn't**/He**'s not** going to go.
>
> We **aren't**/We**'re not** going to go.

1. Affirmative Statements with *Be Going To*

Write affirmative statements with *be going to.* Use the subject + verb in parentheses. Use full forms.

1. (he/get) Charlie is in a Driver's Ed class. <u>He is going to get</u> his driver's license.

2. (I/be) I'm making plans. _____ a college student next year.

3. (it/be) It doesn't look like rain. _____ clear and sunny today.

4. (you/love) I went to that movie last night. It's great! _____ it.

5. (we/have) We are ordering a pizza. _____ pizza for supper tonight.

6. (you/be) Hurry! _____ late!

Talking the Talk

The *going to* in sentences with *be going to* often sounds like "gonna."

WRITE	YOU WILL OFTEN HEAR
They are going to win.	They're "gonna" win.

2. Affirmative and Negative Statements with *Be Going To*

A. What are these people's plans for their futures? Write affirmative statements with *be going to* + *be* and the words in the box. Write full forms.

> a nurse
>
> doctors
>
> lawyers
>
> computer technicians
>
> a chef   an auto mechanic

1. Richard is learning to fix cars. He <u>is going to be an auto mechanic</u> .

2. Randy is going to cooking school. He _____ .

3. Jess and Ron are going to law school. They _____ .

4. Helen is going to nursing school. She _____ .

5. Bruce and I are learning to fix computers. We _____ .

6. Neil and Lucy are going to medical school. They _____ .

B. Work with a partner. Make negative statements about the people in Part A. What AREN'T they going to do? Use contractions.

Example   *Student A:*   Richard isn't going to be an astronaut.

C. Tell your partner three things you aren't going to do in your future.

Example   *Student A:*   I'm not going to go to cooking school.

GRAMMAR BRIEFING 2

Future Time Expressions

USING FUTURE TIME EXPRESSIONS

1. **A future time expression** can come at the beginning or end of a sentence.

> **Tomorrow** she's going to get married.
>
> She's going to get married **tomorrow**.

2. Use *tomorrow + morning, afternoon, evening,* or *night.*

> I'm going to leave **tomorrow morning**.

3. Use *in* + an amount of time.

> He's going to be back **in a few minutes/in an hour/in two weeks**.

4. Use *next* + a period of time.

> We're going to leave **next Friday/next month/next summer**.

3. Future Time Expressions

Write *tomorrow, next,* or *in.*

1. Susie is a senior in high school in Boston. She's going to graduate __next__
   a

   spring. She's going to be a college student _____ year. Now, she's thinking
   b

   about colleges. _____ , she's going to visit some colleges in Boston.
   c

   _____ morning at 10:00, she's going to be at Boston University.
   d

2. It's 9:00. Susie is going to leave her house _____ a few minutes. She needs to
   a

   be at Boston University _____ an hour. She's going to visit Simmons College
   b

   this afternoon and Tufts University _____ afternoon. _____
   c   d

   weekend, she's going to visit colleges in Philadelphia and New York.

4. Future Time Expressions

A. Work in a group. Ask about people's future plans. Ask *When are you going to . . . ?*

QUESTIONS		ANSWERS
have lunch	finish school	*in* + (how much time?)
see a movie	see your family	*next* + (a specific period of time)
take a vacation	_____	*tomorrow (morning, afternoon, evening, night)*
get married	_____	

B. Report to the class. Make two statements about each person in your group.

GRAMMAR BRIEFING 3

Yes/No Questions with *Be Going To*

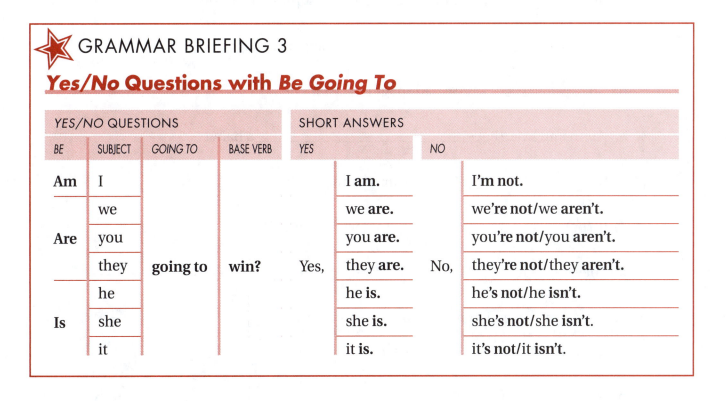

BE	SUBJECT	GOING TO	BASE VERB		YES		NO	
Am	I					I **am.**		I'm not.
	we					we **are.**		we're not/we aren't.
Are	you					you **are.**		you're not/you aren't.
	they	**going to**	**win?**	Yes,		they **are.**	No,	they're not/they aren't.
	he					he **is.**		he's not/he isn't.
Is	she					she **is.**		she's not/she isn't.
	it					it **is.**		it's not/it isn't.

5. *Yes/No* Questions and Short Answers

Write questions with *be going to.* Complete the short answers.

1. *A:* (it/rain) __Is it going to rain__ today?

          a

    B: Yes, __it is__ . (you/do) _____ a lot of walking?

          b   c

    A: Yes, _____ . But it's OK—I have an umbrella.

          d

2. *A:* (your son/go) _____ away to college?

                          a

    B: No, _____ . He has other plans.

          b

    A: (he/get) _____ a job?

                      c

    B: Yes, _____ . And he's going to take some college courses, too.

          d

3. *A:* (we/have) _____ spaghetti tonight?

                      a

    B: No, _____ . We had spaghetti last night.

          b

4. *A:* (Lynn and Evan/have) _____ a baby?

                                  a

    B: Yes, _____ ! In about six months.

          b

    A: (it/be) _____ a boy or a girl?

                      c

    B: They don't know.

5. *A:* Excuse me, Doctor, but (I/need)

    _____ a shot?

              a

    B: Yes, _____ . (you/be) _____

          b   c

    a brave boy?

    A: I don't know. (it/hurt) _____ much?

                              d

    B: No, _____ . It's just going to hurt for a minute.

          e

6. Are *You Going to . . . ?* Questions and Answers

Working in a group, make a list of ten things a person can do with $10,000,000.

1. travel around the world _____
2. _____
3. _____
4. _____
5. _____

6. _____
7. _____
8. _____
9. _____
10. _____

Student A: You are "the winner." Choose two things from the list. Do not tell your choices!
Other students: Guess Student A's choices by asking questions. Take turns playing "the winner."

Example   *Student B:* Are you going to travel around the world?

Student A: Yes, I am. OK, that's one. Next question?

Student C: Are you going to buy a lot of jewelry?

★ GRAMMAR BRIEFING 4

Wh- Questions with *Be Going To*

WH- QUESTIONS						ANSWERS
WH- QUESTION WORD	BE	SUBJECT	GOING TO	BASE VERB		
When	am	I		see	you?	In a week.
Where	are	we/you/they	going to	live?		In New York.
What	is	he/she/it		do?		Who knows?!

7. Answering *Wh-* Questions

Read the news article. Write answers to the *wh-* questions.

New College to Open in Massachusetts

NEEDHAM—A new college is going to open in Needham, Massachusetts. It's going to be called Olin College. It's going to be a college of engineering.

Jack Higgins is a high school senior. He's going to graduate next spring. In the fall, he hopes to go to Olin College. This college is his first choice. He wants to study engin-eering. "Olin College is going to be different," he says. "Olin students are going to be the engineers of the future."

The people at Olin want to change the education of engineers. They are going to try new ideas. You can learn more about it at www.olin.edu.

engineering = the work of planning things like roads and bridges, or planning the design of machines such as computers. (*He's studying engineering.*)

1. What is going to open in Needham, Massachusetts? _a new college_____

2. What is its name going to be? _____

3. What kind of college is it going to be? _____

4. When is Jack Higgins going to finish high school?_____

5. When is he going to go to college? _____

6. What is he going to study? _____

7. Who are going to be "the engineers of the future"? _____

8. What are the people at Olin going to do? _____

8. Forming *Wh-* Questions

A. Write questions with *be going to* and the words in parentheses.

1. (where/you/work) _Where are you going to work?_____

2. (what/you/do) _____

3. (when/you/start) _____

4. (how/you/get to work every day) _____

5. (how much money/you/make) _____

B. Work in a group. Student A: Soon, you are going to finish college and start work. Choose a job from the list, or think of a different job. The others in the group are your family. They are going to ask you *wh-* questions about your job. Take turns.

Example   *Student B:* So, what are you going to do after college?

　　　　　Student A: I'm going to work at Disney World.

a pizza maker at *Mama's Pizza Place*	a taxi driver in Cairo
a nurse at City Hospital	a dancing mouse at Disney World in Florida
a computer engineer in Tokyo	_____

9. *Wh-* Questions and Answers

Work with a partner. What are you looking forward to? Tell your partner about something nice in your future. Ask your partner *wh-* questions about his or her future. Answer your partner's questions. Tell the class about your partner.

Example   *Student A:* I am looking forward to seeing my friends.

　　　　　Student B: When are you going to see them?

EXTRA PRACTICE

10. Negative Statements with *Be Going To*

A. Complete the sentences. Use full forms of *be + not + going to.*

1. He called us last night, so <u>he is not going to call us</u> _____ tonight.

2. I washed my hair this morning, so _____ tonight.

3. They cleaned their apartment yesterday, so _____ today.

4. We bought milk this morning, so _____ this afternoon.

5. She had a hamburger for lunch, so _____ for dinner.

6. You made that mistake once, so _____ again.

B. Underline the subject + *be* + *not* in Part A 1–6. Write contractions. Write two contractions when you can.

         he's not/he isn't

Example . . . , so <u>he is not</u> going to call us **tonight.**

11. Affirmative Statements with Future Time Expressions

On a piece of paper, write eight affirmative statements about people's future plans—your own plans, or the plans of your friends or family. Use *be going to* and these future time expressions: *in* (+ how much time?), *next,* and *tomorrow.*

Examples   I'm going to buy a car in a year.

               My brother is going to visit me next weekend.

12. *Yes/No* Questions with *Be Going To*

Write *yes/no* questions and short answers.

1. it/rain (yes) _Is it going to rain? Yes, it is._____

2. we/need our books (no) _____

3. he/call me back (yes) _____

4. you/come with us (yes) _____

5. they/buy a house (no) _____

6. it/be sunny (yes) _____

7. you and Ahmed/take that course (yes) _____

8. the store/stay open late (no) _____

9. your brother/call you (no) _____

10. I/see the doctor (yes) _____

13. *Yes/No* Questions with *Be Going To*

Think of five famous people. Write their names in a list, from 1 to 5. Write a question to ask each one of them. Use *be going to.*

Example To the President: Are you going to run for re-election?

14. *Wh-* Questions with *Be Going To*

Your friend is leaving school. What are your friend's future plans? On a piece of paper, write five *wh-* questions with *be going to* to ask him or her.

Example What are you going to do next?

CHAPTER 14 Plans and Predictions

GRAMMAR IN ACTION

Reading and Listening

A. Listen and read.

Narrator: Johnny Scott is talking to his sister Janelle on the phone. He's at home, and she's at college. Johnny has a problem, and he wants her help.

Johnny: Janelle, listen, I have to talk to you. I decided something last night. I'm going to go to music school next year.

Janelle: Good for you! I know you never really wanted to be a doctor.

Johnny: But what'll I do? I can't tell Mom and Dad. They'll kill me!

Janelle: No, they won't. They'll understand.

Johnny: Will you tell them?

Janelle: No, Johnny, you have to do it. But don't worry, it'll be fine.

Johnny: Janelle!

Janelle: OK, maybe they won't like it at first. Dad will probably need a little time . . . OK, Johnny, wait and tell them when I get home. We'll do it together.

Johnny: When will you be here?

Janelle: Next week.

B. Work with a partner. Practice the conversation in Part A.

Think about Grammar

A. Find the sentence in Part A with the same meaning. Write it.

1. But what am I going to do? = _But what'll I do?_

2. They're going to understand. = _____

3. But don't worry, it's going to be fine. = _____

4. OK, maybe they aren't going to like it at first. = _____

5. When are you going to be here? = _____

   The contracted form of *will* is _____ .

   The contracted form of *will* + *not* is _____ .

B. Work with a partner. What do these sentences from the conversation mean? Choose a or b.

1. "They'll kill me!"
   a. I expect they are going to be angry at me.
   b. They have a plan to kill me.

2. "Will you tell them?"
   a. Are you going to tell them about my idea?
   b. Will you please tell them for me?

3. "Dad will probably need a little time."
   a. I am 100% sure that he's going to need time (to think about this).
   b. I am 80–90% sure that he's going to need time (to think about this).

C. Work with a partner. Answer the following questions. Predict what is going to happen. Then share your ideas with the class.

1. Will Johnny tell his parents about his decision?

2. Will Janelle help her brother?

3. What will their mother and father say? How will they feel?

GRAMMAR BRIEFING 1

Expressing the Future with *Will*

A. AFFIRMATIVE STATEMENTS

SUBJECT	WILL	BASE VERB	PRONOUN + WILL	BASE VERB
I			I'll	
We			We'll	
You			You'll	
They	will	work.	They'll	work.
He			He'll	
She			She'll	
It			It'll	

B. NEGATIVE STATEMENTS

SUBJECT	WILL NOT	BASE VERB	SUBJECT	WON'T	BASE VERB
I			I		
We			We		
You			You		
They	will not	work.	They	won't	work.
He			He		
She			She		
It			It		

C. FUNCTION OF WILL

Use *will* (or *be going to*) to make predictions about the future.

I'm sure you**'ll** win/you**'re going to** win.

It **won't** rain./It**'s not going to** rain.

1. Statements with *Will (Not)*

A. These sentences are predictions about Johnny, Janelle, and their parents (page 232). Rewrite them with *will.* Use full forms, not contractions.

1. *Johnny:* They are going to kill me! ___They will kill me!_____

2. He is going to wait for his sister. _____

3. She is going to help him. _____

4. She is going to be home next week. _____

5. They are going to talk to their parents. _____

6. It is going to be a serious conversation. _____

B. Underline the full forms in Part A. Write contractions.

They'll
Example   <u>They will</u> kill me!

C. Write three negative statements with *won't.* Write predictions about Johnny, Janelle, or their parents.

Example   Johnny's parents won't like his plans.

1. _____

2. _____

3. _____

2. Affirmative and Negative Statements with *Will*

A. Listen to the forecast (predictions about the weather). Draw pictures or write words for the weather each day (for example, *sunny, cloudy, rainy*).

Monday	Tuesday	Wednesday	Thursday	Friday
cloudy				

B. Work with a partner. Tell the five-day forecast from Part A. Use *will* and *won't.* Then share predictions about the weather in your area.

⭐ GRAMMAR BRIEFING 2

Questions with *Will*

A. *YES/NO* QUESTIONS

QUESTIONS			SHORT ANSWERS				
WILL	SUBJECT	BASE VERB		YES		NO	
Will	I / we / you / they / he / she / it	be	on time?	Yes,	I / we / you / they / he / she / it will.	No,	I / we / you / they / he / she / it won't.

B. *WH*-QUESTIONS

QUESTIONS					ANSWERS
WH- QUESTION WORD	WILL	SUBJECT	BASE VERB		
What	will	the weather	be	like?	Clear and sunny.
Where	will	they	play	the game?	At the new stadium.
What time	will	the game	start?		At 4:00.
How much	will	tickets	cost?		$25.00.

💬 Talking the Talk

Use *Will you* to ask for something.
  (Do not use *Are you going to.*)

A: **Will you** help me?
  NOT: ~~Are you going to~~ help me?

B: Sure! (OR: I'm sorry, but I can't.)

3. Asking for Something with *Will You*

A. Work with a partner. Write the two conversations. Use *Will you* to ask for something.

B. With your partner, act out your conversations for the class.

4. *Yes/No* Questions and Short Answers with *Will*

A. Read the information about the 2008 Olympic Games. Write five *yes/no* questions and their short answers.

We will have Olympic Games in the year 2008. China will host the Games. These will be the Summer Games. They won't have any winter sports. Athletes will come from 200 countries. They will try to win their events. Some events of the Summer Games are swimming, basketball, and soccer. It will be an exciting time!

1. Will we have Olympic Games in 2008? Yes, we will. _____

2. _____

3. _____

4. _____

5. _____

B. Work with a partner. Ask your questions from Part A. Answer your partner's questions. Write one more question about the Games. Ask the class.

5. *Wh-* Questions and Answers with *Will*

A. Put the words in order. Write *wh-* questions about the 2008 Olympics. Add *will*.

1. the 2008 Olympic Games/where/be _Where will the 2008 Olympic Games be?_____

2. when/take place/the Games _____

3. they/what sports/have _____

4. see/we/who/at the games _____

5. what/try to do/the athletes _____

B. Work with a partner. Ask and answer the questions from Part A. (Look back at exercise 4 if you need information.) Write two more *wh-* questions about future Olympic Games. Ask the class.

Example   *Where will the next Winter Olympic Games take place?*

★ GRAMMAR BRIEFING 3

Will vs. *Be going to*

FUNCTIONS OF *WILL* AND *BE GOING TO*

1. Remember! Both *will* and *be going to* can be used in predictions.

> **You'll do** well on the test.
>
> **You're going to do** well on the test.

2. Use *I'm going to* (usually not *I will*) to tell your plans for the future.

> **I'm going to go** shopping this weekend.

Talking the Talk

Use *I'll* or *We'll* to offer to do something. (Do not use *I'm/We're going to*.)

> *A:* **I'll** pass out the books.
> *B:* Thank you!
>
> *A:* Can someone help me with this?
> *B:* Sure, **we'll** help you.

6. Offering to Do Something

A. Write the offers of help. Use *I'll* or *We'll* + the words in parentheses.

1. (open it for you)

2. (show you)

3. (do it)

4. (give you a ride)

B. Work with a partner. Student A: Tell a problem you have. Student B: Offer to help. Take turns.

7. Making Predictions and Telling Plans

A. Write statements.

1. Make predictions about the weather.

   (*will*) _____

   (*be going to*) _____

2. Make predictions about the class or your classmates.

   (*will*) _____

   (*be going to*) _____

3. Tell your plans for tonight.

(*be going to*) _____

4. Tell your plans for this weekend.

(*be going to*) _____

B. Share your predictions with a partner. Do you agree? Tell your plans. Are they the same or different?

 GRAMMAR BRIEFING 4

Have To

A. AFFIRMATIVE STATEMENTS

SUBJECT	HAVE/HAS TO	BASE VERB
I / We / You / They	**have to**	**leave.**
He / She / It	**has to**	

B. MEANING

1. Use *have to* when something is necessary. (Someone needs to do it and has no choice.)

> Movies aren't free. You **have to pay.** You **have to buy** a ticket, or you can't go in.

2. *Have to* can have present or future meaning.

PRESENT MEANING	FUTURE MEANING
I **have to study** every day.	I **have to study** next weekend.

Talking the Talk

In conversation, *have to* often sounds like "hafta." *Has to* often sounds like "hasta."

WRITE	YOU WILL OFTEN HEAR
I **have to** go now.	I "hafta" go now.
She **has to** work at 9:00.	She "hasta" work at 9:00.

8. Affirmative Statements with *Have to*

Complete the statements with *have to* or *has to*.

1. The doctor says _you have to take this medicine._____
                    you/take this medicine

2. The store is closing, so _____ soon.
                             we/leave

3. His car isn't working, so _____
                              he/take the bus

4 A: Do you have time to talk now?

   B: Sorry, but I can't. _____
                           I/go to work

5. A: Can Kerry come with us?

   B: No, _____ tonight.
            she/study

6. The law says that _____
                      children/go to school

7. _____ before you can drive a car.
    you/get a license

8. Jerry is graduating from school. Now _____
                                        he/find a job

9. Affirmative Statements with *Have to*

A. Janelle is a college student. It's time for her to register for classes for next semester. Listen to the information about registering for classes. Listen again and check (✓) the things Janelle has to do.

1. _✓_ choose courses for next semester
2. ____ talk to other students
3. ____ buy a course catalogue
4. ____ use her computer to read about the courses online
5. ____ make an appointment with her advisor
6. ____ call her advisor to make the appointment
7. ____ talk about her course choices with her advisor
8. ____ fill out a course registration form
9. ____ take the form to the Registrar's Office

> **ADVISING APPOINTMENTS**
> *PROF. YEE*
>
> Monday
>
> 8:00 *Joel Simmons* _____
>
> 8:15 *Mike Herrera* _____
>
> 8:30 _____
>
> 8:45 *Emily Watanabe* _____
>
> 9:00 _____
>
> 9:15 _____
>
> Tuesday
>
> 2:00 _____

register for a class = put your name on the list of people taking a course (*High school and college students have to register for classes.*)

> COURSE REGISTRATION FORM
>
> Semester _____ Year _____
> Name _____
> Student ID _____
> Courses:
>
> _____   _____
> _____   _____
> _____   _____
>
> Advisor's signature _____

B. Work with a partner. Tell the things Janelle has to do. Take turns.

Example   *Student A:* She has to choose courses.

10. Using *Have To*

Work in a group. What does a person have to do to get into this course (the course you are taking)? Make a list. Use *You have to.*

Example   You have to get information from. . . .

EXTRA PRACTICE

11. Negative Statements with *Will*

A. Rewrite these statements with *will*. Use full forms, not contractions.

1. I am not going to be late. _I will not be late._____

2. It is not going to hurt. _____

3. You are not going to need a jacket. _____

4. He is not going to win the race. _____

5. We are not going to have much time. _____

6. They are not going to be here tomorrow. _____

7. She is not going to get the job. _____

B. Underline each *will not* + verb in Part A. Write the contraction + verb.

 Example   won't be
         I <u>will not be</u> late.

12. Questions with *Will*

A. Write *yes/no* questions and short answers. Use *will*.

1. I/need warm clothes (no) _Will I need warm clothes? No, you won't._____

2. the trip/be expensive (yes) _____

3. trains/arrive on time (yes) _____

4. you/ be careful (yes) _____

5. she/come with us (no) _____

B. Write *wh-* questions with *will*. The **boldfaced** words are the answers.

1. Professor Yee will teach **Biology 120.** _What will Professor Yee teach?_____

2. They'll be **at the beach** next weekend. _____

3. The party will be **on Saturday.** _____

4. He'll do it **because he has to.** _____

5. I'll bring **some photos** to class. _____

13. *Will* vs. *Be Going To*

A. Match each type of statement with an example.

_____ 1. A prediction about the future   a. I'm going to study engineering next year.

_____ 2. A future plan   b. I'll wait for you.

_____ 3. An offer to do something   c. It's going to rain tomorrow.

B. Write ten statements on a piece of paper.

1. Write four predictions (about sports, a famous person, the weather, or someone in your class). Use *will* in two statements, and use *be going to* in two statements.

2. Write three statements about your future plans. Use *be going to.*

3. Make three offers. Write what you are offering to do and for whom. Use *will.*

Example 3. a. To my mother: I'll do the dishes.

14. *Have To*

Complete the statements. Use *have to* or *has to.*

1. I can't go to the movies tonight because I _____

2. Marie needs a job. She _____

3. They can't stay. They _____

4. The doctor says I _____

5. Yusef wants to go to a good college, so he _____

6. Mikhail needs to know English, so he _____

15. *I Have To*

On a piece of paper, write four statements with *have to.*

1. Write a statement about something you always have to do.

2. Write a statement about something you sometimes have to do.

3. Write two statements about things you have to do in the future (and when).

Example I always have to show my student ID at the library.

Unit 7 Wrap-Up Activities

1. Waiting and Wondering: READING

Read this paragraph.

> Next Monday will be April 15. It's going to be a big day for people like me: high school seniors all over the United States. Why? We are waiting for letters from colleges. Months ago, we visited colleges, we made decisions about our futures, and we sent our college applications. Now, we have to wait. Everybody is wondering, "Will I get in?" I really want to study music at the University of Southern California. But are they going to accept me? Maybe they will, and maybe they won't. I'm going to find out on Monday.

2. A Special Day in Your Future: WRITING

Are you looking forward to a special day in your future? Why? What's going to happen? When will this be? Write about it. (Remember: when you write about future plans, use *I am going to*, not *I will*.)

3. Looking Forward to a Visit: EDITING

Correct the nine errors. The first one is corrected for you.

    I'm looking forward to tomorrow. My friend Yu-Kyung ~~will~~ *is* going to visit me. She going to come in tomorrow afternoon, and she's will spend three days here. We going to have a lot of fun. We'll to visit different places, go shopping, and go out to eat. Tonight I have to calling her. We has to make plans to meet at the airport. I'm have to clean my room, too!

4. Future Plans: SPEAKING/LISTENING

Read the statements in the chart. Walk around and ask your classmates *Are you going to...?* After each *yes* answer, ask for more information. Use a *wh-* question. Write notes about people's answers.

1. ___Sonia___ is going to take a trip.

2. _____ is going to have fun on the weekend.

3. _____ is going to buy something.

4. _____ is going to meet a friend later.

5. _____ is going to look for a job.

NOTES
1. *Dallas*
2.
3.
4.
5.

5. Madame X Knows All: WRITING/SPEAKING/LISTENING

Step One: You are going to visit the Great and Powerful Madame X. She makes predictions about the future. Write three *wh-* questions with *will* on three pieces of paper. Sign your name. You can ask about your future, your friends, or world events.

Example   Who will I marry? Katya

When will my country win the World Cup?
Jorge—Mexico

Step Two: Form a group. Put all the questions from your group in an envelope. Student A is Madame X. Another student picks a question and reads it. Madame X will answer. Take turns.

Example   *Student B:* "Who will I marry?" Katya wants to know.

Madame X: Katya will marry a rich man from Texas. He will be tall, dark, and handsome. They will have seven children. . . .

GRAMMAR SUMMARY

Future Time Expressions

I'm going to leave **in a few minutes.**

I'll see you **next Monday.**

★ See the Grammar Briefing on page 224.

Expressing the Future with *Be Going To*

STATEMENTS

I	am		
We/You/They	are	(not) going to	be here.
He/She/It	is		

QUESTIONS AND ANSWERS

Am	I		Yes, you **are.**	No, you**'re not.**
Are	you	going to be on time?	Yes, I **am.**	No, I**'m not.**
Is	it		Yes, it **is.**	No, it's **not.**

What are you **going to do?**	I'm going to go to the game.
Where is it **going to be?**	At the stadium.

★ See the Grammar Briefings on pages 222, 225, 227, and 238.

Expressing the Future with *Will*

STATEMENTS

I/We/You/They/He/She/It **will (not) be** late.

QUESTIONS AND ANSWERS

Will I/we/you/they/he/she/it **do** a good job?   Yes, I **will.**   No, I **won't.**

What will the weather **be** like?	Nice and warm.
Why will you **need** an umbrella?	Because it will probably rain.

★ See the Grammar Briefings on pages 234, 236, and 238.

Have To

I/We/You/They **have to register** for courses next week.

He/She/It **has to go** now.

★ See the Grammar Briefing on page 240.

TEST YOURSELF ON CHAPTER 13

1. Write affirmative statements with *be going to.* Use contractions.

1. (he/talk/to his friend) He's going to talk to his friend.
2. (they/study/at the library) _____
3. (we/go/to a party) _____
4. (you/need/more information) _____
5. (it/rain/soon) _____
6. (I/watch/the news on TV) _____

2. Rewrite statements 1, 2, 4, and 6 from Part 1. Make them negative. Use contractions.

1. He's not going to talk to his friend./He isn't going to talk to his friend.
2. _____
3. _____
4. _____

3. Write *yes/no* questions with *be going to.* Write the short answers.

1. you/see him later (yes) Are you going to see him later? Yes, I am.
2. we/have class tomorrow (no) _____
3. he/call a doctor (yes) _____
4. it/going to hurt (no) _____

4. Write *wh-* questions with *be going to.* The **boldfaced** words are the answers.

1. The train is going to leave **at 10:10.** When is the train going to leave?
2. They are going to work **in Spain.** _____
3. I am going to call **my brother.** _____
4. Lunch is going to cost **$10.00.** _____

5. Find the six errors and correct them.

1. We're going to meet ~~in~~ tomorrow.

2. I am going to see the movie last Friday.

3. She will going to call me.

4. When you are going to come back?

5. The show is going to start a few minutes.

6. They going to buy a new car.

TEST YOURSELF ON CHAPTER 14

6. Rewrite the statements with *will* (+ *not*). Use contractions.

1. It is going to be hot all weekend. It'll be hot all weekend. _____

2. Maybe he is going to call. _____

3. You are not going to have any trouble. _____

4. She is going to have her baby in May. _____

5. I am not going to need a coat. _____

6. They are going to win the game. _____

7. Write *wh-* questions with *will*. The boldfaced words are the answers.

1. The weather will be **cold.** How will the weather be? _____

2. Class will begin **in five minutes.** _____

3. The group will meet **in Room 112.** _____

4. They will buy **clothes** at the mall. _____

8. Choose *will* or *be going to*.

1. *A:* Help! How do I turn on this computer? *B:* (I'll/I'm going to) show you.

2. *A:* What are your plans for tonight? *B:* (I'll/I'm going to) see a movie.

3. *A:* I can't open this jar. (Will you/Are you going to) do it for me? *B:* Sure.

9. Write *have to* or *has to*.

1. Can Luis come to the party? No, he _____ work that night.

2. My watch is broken, so I _____ get a new watch.

3. We can't park here. We _____ move the car.

4. Fahima's son is sick. She _____ take him to the doctor.

10. Find the six errors and correct them.

1. You'll ~~going to~~ have fun.

2. I will to see you later.

3. She's will call me tonight.

4. You has to be there at 8:10.

5. They'll not be here tomorrow.

6. When you will do it?

See Answer Key pages ANS-7 and ANS-8.

Appendixes

APPENDIX 1

Numbers

CARDINAL NUMBERS	ORDINAL NUMBERS	CARDINAL NUMBERS	ORDINAL NUMBERS
1 = one	1st = first	11 = eleven	11th = eleventh
2 = two	2nd = second	12 = twelve	12th = twelfth
3 = three	3rd = third	13 = thirteen	13th = thirteenth
4 = four	4th = fourth	14 = fourteen	14th = fourteenth
5 = five	5th = fifth	15 = fifteen	15th = fifteenth
6 = six	6th = sixth	16 = sixteen	16th = sixteenth
7 = seven	7th = seventh	17 = seventeen	17th = seventeenth
8 = eight	8th = eighth	18 = eighteen	18th = eighteenth
9 = nine	9th = ninth	19 = nineteen	19th = nineteenth
10 = ten	10th = tenth	20 = twenty	20th = twentieth

CARDINAL NUMBERS	ORDINAL NUMBERS
21 = twenty-one	21st = twenty-first
30 = thirty	30th = thirtieth
40 = forty	40th = fortieth
50 = fifty	50th = fiftieth
60 = sixty	60th = sixtieth
70 = seventy	70th = seventieth
80 = eighty	80th = eightieth
90 = ninety	90th = ninetieth
100 = one hundred	100th = one hundredth
200 = two hundred	200th = two hundredth
1,000 = one thousand	1,000th = one thousandth
1,000,000 = one million	1,000,000th = one millionth

APPENDIX 2

The Days of the Week

WEEKDAYS		THE WEEKEND	
Monday	Mon./M	Saturday	Sat./S
Tuesday	Tues./T	Sunday	Sun./Su
Wednesday	Wed./W		
Thursday	Thurs./Th		
Friday	Fri./F		

The Months of the Year

1	January	Jan.	7	July	Jul.
2	February	Feb.	8	August	Aug.
3	March	Mar.	9	September	Sept.
4	April	Apr.	10	October	Oct.
5	May		11	November	Nov.
6	June	Jun.	12	December	Dec.

Dates

In the United States, people write dates as "(month)/(day)" or "(month)/(day)/(year)."

10/1 = October 1

1/10/05 = January 10, 2005

The day is before the month in "the Fourth of July" and "the 31st of October."

APPENDIX 3

Spelling Rules for Plural Count Nouns

1. Most nouns: Add -*s*.

    student → students   radio → radios   day → days   shoe → shoes

2. Nouns ending in *ch, sh, ss,* or *x:* Add -*es*.

    watch → watches   dish → dishes   class → classes   box → boxes

3. Most nouns ending in *o:* Add -*es*.

    potato → potatoes   tomato → tomatoes

    Some nouns add -*s* only:

    radio → radios   video → videos

4. Nouns ending in a consonant + *y:* Drop the *y* and add -*ies*.

    family → families   dictionary → dictionaries

5. Some nouns ending in *f* or *fe:* Drop the *f* or *fe* and add -*ves*.

    wife → wives   knife → knives   leaf → leaves

Irregular Plurals

person/people   man/men   woman/women   child/children   foot/feet   tooth/teeth

Nouns with Only a Plural Form

clothes, pants, jeans, shorts, (eye)glasses, sunglasses

APPENDIX 4

Some Common Noncount Nouns

LIQUIDS	SOLIDS	THINGS WITH PARTICLES	GROUPS OF SIMILAR THINGS
coffee	bread	cereal	clothing
juice	butter	corn	food
milk	cheese	dirt	fruit
oil	gold	dust	furniture
soda	ice	rice	jewelry
soup	meat	salt	money
tea	plastic	sand	
water	wood	sugar	

WEATHER	SCHOOL SUBJECTS	ABSTRACT IDEAS	OTHER
fog	business	advice	air
lightning	English	education	mail
rain	history	fun	music
snow	math	information	smoke
weather	science	love	traffic
		work	

APPENDIX 5

Spelling of –ing Verbs

1. Most verbs: Add *-ing* to the **base form of the verb.**

    go → go**ing**   wear → wear**ing**   carry → carry**ing**

2. Verbs that end in *ie:* Change the *ie* to *y,* and add *-ing.*

    lie → l**ying**   die → d**ying**

3. Verbs that end in a consonant* + *e:* Drop the *e,* and add *-ing.*

    writ**e** → writ**ing**   tak**e** → tak**ing**

4. For most verbs that end in "C V C" (consonant + vowel + consonant):

    Double the final consonant and add *-ing:*

    cut → cu**tting**   begin → begi**nning**

    BUT:

    • Do not double *w* or *x:* sno**wing**   fi**xing**

    • Do not double the final consonant when the last syllable is not stressed:

Last Syllable Stressed	Last Syllable Not Stressed
. ●	● .
be-*GIN* → begi**nning**	*LIS*-ten → listening

* See page 2 for the consonants and vowels.

APPENDIX 6

Spelling Rules for Present Tense Third Person Singular Verbs

1. Most verbs: Add -*s*.

    eat → eat**s**   drink → drink**s**   play → play**s**

2. Verbs ending in *ch, sh, ss,* or *x:* Add -*es*.

    wat**ch** → watch**es**   wa**sh** → wash**es**   ki**ss** → kiss**es**   mi**x** → mix**es**

3. Verbs ending in a consonant + *y:* Drop the *y* and add -*ies*.

    stud**y** → stud**ies**   carr**y** → carr**ies**

4. Irregular verbs: have → **has**   go → **goes**   do → **does**

Pronunciation of the Final –s on Third Person Singular Verbs

There are three ways to pronounce the -*s* ending on present tense verbs.

1. Add the syllable /ɪz/ when the base verb ends in /s/, /z/, /sh/, /ch/, /zh/, /j/, or /ks/.

    kisses /KISS ɪz/   buzzes, washes, matches, massages, judges, fixes

2. Say /s/ when the base verb ends in voiceless sounds such as /k/, /p/, /t/, and /f/.

    picks, jumps, cuts, laughs (gh = / f /)

3. Say /z/ for all other -*s* verb endings.

APPENDIX 7

Spelling Rules for Forming the Simple Past Tense of Regular Verbs

Add *-(e)d* to the base form of a regular verb for the simple past tense form.

1. Most verbs: Add *-ed.*

   watch → watch**ed**   play → play**ed**   pick up → pick**ed** up

2. Verbs that end in *e:* Add *-d.*

   smil**e** → smil**ed**   danc**e** → danc**ed**

3. Verbs that end in a consonant* + *y:* Drop the *y* and add *-ied.*

   stud**y** → stud**ied**   tr**y** → tr**ied**

4. For most regular verbs that end in "C V C," double the final consonant and add *-ed.*

   hug → hug**ged**   **rob** → rob**bed**   cont**rol** → contro**lled**

   BUT:

   • Do not double *w* or *x:* snow**ed**   fix**ed**

   • Do not double the final consonant when the last syllable is not stressed:

Last Syllable Stressed	Last Syllable NOT Stressed
• ●	● •
permit → permi**tted**	listen → listen**ed**

* See page 2 for the consonants and vowels.

Pronunciation of Simple Past –ed Endings

There are three ways to pronounce the *-ed* ending on regular verbs in the simple past.

1. Add the syllable /ɪd/ when the base verb ends in the sound /t/ or /d.

   want, wanted   load, loaded   pretend, pretended

2. Say /t/ when the base verb ends in the voiceless sound /f/, /k/, /p/, /s/, /ch/, /sh/, or /ks/.

   laughed (gh = /f/), picked, jumped, kissed, watched, washed, fixed

3. Say /d/ for all other *-ed* verb endings.

APPENDIX 8

Some Common Irregular Verbs

BASE FORM	SIMPLE PAST FORM	BASE FORM	SIMPLE PAST FORM	BASE FORM	SIMPLE PAST FORM
be	was, were	get	got	run	ran
begin	began	give	gave	say	said
break	broke	go	went	see	saw
bring	brought	grow	grew	send	sent
build	built	have	had	sing	sang
buy	bought	hear	heard	sit	sat
come	came	hit	hit	sleep	slept
cost	cost	hurt	hurt	speak	spoke
cut	cut	know	knew	spend	spent
do	did	leave	left	stand	stood
drink	drank	lose	lost	take	took
drive	drove	make	made	tell	told
eat	ate	mean	meant	think	thought
fall	fell	meet	met	understand	understood
feel	felt	pay	paid	wake up	woke up
find	found	put	put	wear	wore
fly	flew	read	read	win	won
forget	forgot	ride	rode	write	wrote

APPENDIX 9

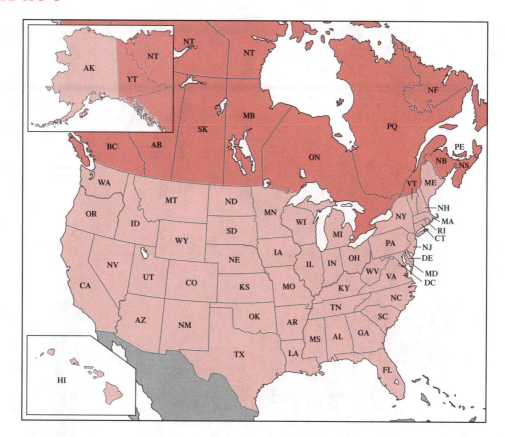

Names and Abbreviations of the 50 States

AL	Alabama	IN	Indiana	NE	Nebraska	SC	South Carolina
AK	Alaska	IA	Iowa	NV	Nevada	SD	South Dakota
AZ	Arizona	KS	Kansas	NH	New Hampshire	TN	Tennessee
AR	Arkansas	KY	Kentucky	NJ	New Jersey	TX	Texas
CA	California	LA	Louisiana	NM	New Mexico	UT	Utah
CO	Colorado	ME	Maine	NY	New York	VT	Vermont
CT	Connecticut	MD	Maryland	NC	North Carolina	VA	Virginia
DE	Delaware	MA	Massachusetts	ND	North Dakota	WA	Washington
FL	Florida	MI	Michigan	OH	Ohio	WV	West Virginia
GA	Georgia	MN	Minnesota	OK	Oklahoma	WI	Wisconsin
HI	Hawaii	MS	Mississippi	OR	Oregon	WY	Wyoming
ID	Idaho	MO	Missouri	PA	Pennsylvania	DC*	District of Columbia
IL	Illinois	MT	Montana	RI	Rhode Island		(*not a state)

Names and Abbreviations of the 10 Canadian Provinces and 3 Territories

AB	Alberta	NF	Newfoundland	PE	Prince Edward
BC	British Columbia	NT	Northwest Territories	PQ	Quebec
MB	Manitoba	NS	Nova Scotia	SK	Saskatchewan
NB	New Brunswick	NT	Nunavut	YT	Yukon Territory
		ON	Ontario		

APPENDIX 10

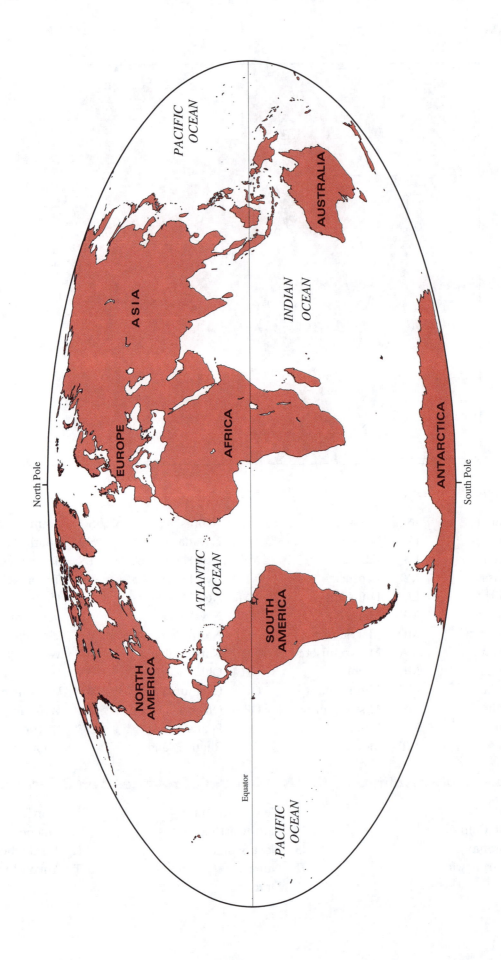

Answer Key— Test Yourself

UNIT 1: TEST YOURSELF ON CHAPTER 1, PAGE 39

1. 2. It
   3. I
   4. you
   5. he
   6. she

2. 2. She's
   3. I'm
   4. You're
   5. It's
   6. He's
   7. She's
   8. It's

3. 2. your
   3. His
   4. her
   5. My
   6. your
   7. His

4. 2. Who is/Who's he?
   3. Where is/Where's the teacher?
   4. What is/What's your name?
   5. Where is/Where's he from?
   6. Where are you from?
   7. What is/what's this? or What is it?

5. 2. You are in my class.
   3. What is your name?
   4. This is Elena. She is my classmate.
   5. Where is/Where's he from?
   6. I am/I'm from Syria.
   7. Mr. Ives is the teacher. He is a good teacher.
   8. You are/You're a good student.

UNIT 1: TEST YOURSELF ON CHAPTER 2, PAGE 40

6. 2. computers
   3. men
   4. erasers
   5. children
   6. women
   7. keys
   8. pictures
   9. classmates
   10. people

7. 2. You're
   3. They're
   4. They're

   5. We're
   6. You're

8. 2. There are
   3. There are
   4. There's

   5. There's
   6. There are

9. 2. this
   3. These
   4. these

   5. These
   6. This

10. 2. Mikhail and I are from Moscow. We are/We're Russian.
    3. These men are from Indonesia.
    4. The students are in class.
    5. What's this?/What are these?
    6. What are their names?
    7. There are five children in my family.
    8. Jad and Monta are from Thailand. They are/They're Thai.

UNIT 2: TEST YOURSELF ON CHAPTER 3, PAGE 73

1. 2. (He)'s not/isn't
   3. (We)'re not/aren't
   4. isn't

   5. aren't
   6. (You)'re not/aren't

2. 1. (I)'m not
   2. Is it, is
   3. Are they,(they)'re not/aren't

   4. Is he, is
   5. Are we,(we)'re not/aren't
   6. Are you, am

3. 2. has
   3. have
   4. has

   5. has
   6. have

4. 2. How many brothers do you have?
   3. Do you have sisters?

   4. How old is he?
   5. How many children do you have?

5. 2. How old is she?
   3. You have a nice car.
   4. Do you have children?

   5. She is not married.
   6. Is he handsome? Yes, he is.

UNIT 2: TEST YOURSELF ON CHAPTER 4, PAGE 74

6. 2. a
   3. an
   4. a
   5. –

6. a
7. –
8. an

7. 2. those
   3. Those
   4. that

5. That
6. Those

8. 2. Phil's car is small.
   3. His eyes are blue.

4. That is a good picture.

9. 2. Mary's
   3. brothers'
   4. people's

5. friend's
6. parents'

10. 2. They're handsome boys.
    3. Those are Mr. Hall's keys.
    4. Here's a picture of my family.
    5. Those are my friends Pavel and Eva.

6. He's a tall boy.
7. That is her husband's car.
8. Those girls have a cat. It's the girls' cat.

UNIT 3: TEST YOURSELF ON CHAPTER 5, PAGE 109

1. 2. The man is carrying a briefcase.
   3. You are making a mistake.

4. The movie is beginning.
5. The children are getting hungry.

2. 2. Is he using the phone? Yes, he is.
   3. Are the boys waiting? No, they're not/they aren't.

3. 2. What is she doing? e. Fixing her car.
   3. What are you wearing? a. Jeans and a T-shirt.
   4. What are they watching? d. A basketball game.
   5. What is he holding? c. A cup of coffee.

4. 2. classes
   3. parties
   4. knives
   5. eyes
   6. faxes

7. teeth
8. leaves
9. babies
10. radios

5. 2. The game is starting now.

    3. Is your friend having a good time?

    4. We're doing homework right now.

    5. My sunglasses are new.

    6. What are you cooking?

UNIT 3: TEST YOURSELF ON CHAPTER 6, PAGE 110

6. 2. My sister and I aren't planning a party.

    3. My wife isn't having a baby.

    4. I'm not thinking about school.

    5. You're not/You aren't listening to me.

7. 2. Oscar can't speak Italian.

    3. Susan can't fix a car.

    4. Oscar can fix a car.

8. 2. Can that man read music? No, he can't.

    3. Can you go to school by bus? Yes, I can.

    4. Can Luisa ride a horse? No, she can't.

9. 2. or

    3. but

    4. and

    5. but

    6. or

10. 2. His girlfriend can speak Spanish.

    3. They're not/They aren't shopping.

    4. We're having pizza and soda.

    5. Can they fix it? No, they can't.

    6. It isn't raining today.

UNIT 4: TEST YOURSELF ON CHAPTER 7, PAGE 147

1. 1. works

    2. flies

    3. carry

    4. says

    5. love

    6. goes

    7. has

    8. have

    9. misses

2. 2. carries

    3. watches

    4. plays

    5. kisses

    6. marries

    7. puts on

    8. finishes

    9. cries

3. 2. Does she cook Chinese food? Yes, she does.

    3. Do they eat meat? No, they don't.

    4. Does the soup need salt? No, it doesn't.

    5. Does he wash the dishes? Yes, he does.

4. 1. is ringing
   2. know

3. are not/aren't listening
4. need

5. 2. I like my classmates.
   3. Does he take the bus every day?
   4. We're doing/We do our homework at the library.

5. He's working/He works at the mall.
6. Do you have a car?

UNIT 4: TEST YOURSELF ON CHAPTER 8, PAGE 148

6. 2. He doesn't enjoy parties.
   3. The flowers don't need more water.

4. She doesn't have lot of homework.
5. You don't listen to me.

7. 2. How often does he have class?
   3. What do you do?

4. Where do they work?

8. 1. The bus doesn't always come on time.
   2. I am usually on time.

3. Tom doesn't often get up early.
4. She never calls me.

9. *A:* Would you like something to drink?
   B: Yes, please. I'd like some coffee.

A: Would you like cream and sugar in it?
B: I'd like just milk, please.

10. 2. Where does he usually eat lunch?
    3. We never eat in restaurants.
    4. How often do you eat ice cream?

5. I'd like some more water, please.
6. She doesn't have a car.

UNIT 5: TEST YOURSELF ON CHAPTER 9, PAGE 183

1. 2. It's Saturday.
   3. It's two o'clock.
   4. It's November 21.

5. It's sunny.
6. It's cloudy.

2. 1. (b) to, (c) for
   2. (a) in, (b) in
   3. (a) on, (b) on

4. (a) in, (b) at
5. (a) at/in, (b) on, (c) between, (d) on

3. 1. him
   2. it
   3. us

4. her
5. them

4. 2. It's/It is a rainy day.
   3. Chris and I like warm weather.
   4. Sang Youn usually sits in back of Juan.

5. The nurse's office is next to the school library.
6. Come here and sit near me.

UNIT 5: TEST YOURSELF ON CHAPTER 10, PAGE 184

5. 1. –
2. –
3. looks

4. is
5. a
6. –

6. 1. –
2. –
3. the

4. –
5. The
6. the

7. 2. Are there a lot of people in your class?
3. Is there a bus at 8:30?

4. Is there good food at that restaurant?

8. 1. *A:* any, *B:* a lot of, a little

2. *A:* How much, *B:* Not much, a lot of

9. 2. People in China eat a lot of rice.
3. I don't have a lot of money.
4. Is there mail for me?

5. There are a few strawberries on the table.
6. He never drinks coffee or tea.

UNIT 6: TEST YOURSELF ON CHAPTER 11, PAGE 217

1. 1. ago
2. last
3. yesterday

4. yesterday
5. ago
6. last

2. 1. was
2. weren't
3. were

4. wasn't
5. were
6. were

3. 2. Where were you at 2:00?   d. In my math class.
3. How was the weather?   e. Great!
4. Was he here on Monday?   a. No, he was absent.
5. Why was he absent?   b. Because he was sick.

4. 2. bought
3. carried
4. saw
5. watched

6. took
7. hugged
8. ate

5. 2. He went to work by bus.
3. You were right, and I was wrong.
4. She did all her homework.

5. The police stopped the driver.
6. When were you at the mall?

UNIT 6: TEST YOURSELF ON CHAPTER 12, PAGE 218

6. 2. Did the movie end at 11:00? Yes, it did.
   3. Did they leave the room? Yes, they did.
   4. Did it arrive on time? No, it didn't.
   5. Did you meet his new girlfriend? Yes, I did.

7. 1. The men didn't rob a bank.   3. He didn't try the door.
   2. I didn't sleep very well.

8. 1. He ran to the gym.   3. Her dog came with her.
   2. Did you read the newspaper?   4. Did he drink much soda?

9. 1. What time/When did the movie begin?   3. Where did they go?
   2. Who/Whom did you call?   4. What did she eat?

10. 2. Where did you go after work?   5. Janez and I didn't drink any coffee.
    3. I didn't buy much at the store.   6. Did he take his medicine?
    4. Did they do all the homework?

UNIT 7: TEST YOURSELF ON CHAPTER 13, PAGE 249

1. 2. They're going to study at the library.   5. It's going to rain soon.
   3. We're going to go to a party.   6. I'm going to watch the news on TV.
   4. You're going to need more information.

2. 2. They're not/They aren't going to study at the library.
   3. You're not/You aren't going to need more information.
   4. I'm not going to watch the news on TV.

3. 2. Are we going to have class tomorrow? No, we/you aren't. *or* No, we're/you're not.
   3. Is he going to call a doctor? Yes, he is.
   4. Is it going to hurt? No, it isn't/it's not.

4. 2. Where are they going to work?   4. How much is lunch going to cost?
   3. Who(m) are you going to call?

5. 2. I am going to see the movie next Friday.   5. The show is going to start in a few minutes.
   3. She is going to call me.   6. They are going to buy a new car.
   4. When are you going to come back?

UNIT 7: TEST YOURSELF ON CHAPTER 14, PAGE 250

6. 2. Maybe he'll call.

   3. You won't have any trouble.

   4. She'll have her baby in May.

   5. I won't need a coat.

   6. They'll win the game.

7. 2. When will class begin?

   3. Where will the group meet?

   4. What will they buy at the mall?

8. 1. I'll

   2. I'm going to

   3. Will you

9. 1. has to

   2. have to

   3. have to

   4. has to

10. 2. I will see you later.

    3. She'll call me tonight./She's going to call me tonight.

    4. You have to be there at 8:10.

    5. They won't be here tomorrow.

    6. When will you do it?

Tapescript

INTRODUCTORY UNIT: USEFUL WORDS AND EXPRESSIONS

Page 1, Hi!

Exercise 1, Part A. Listen and read.

Luz: Hi! I'm Luz.

Yoshi: I'm Yoshi.

Luz: Nice to meet you.

Yoshi: Nice to meet you, too.

Page 2, The Letters of the Alphabet

Exercise 1. Listen and repeat the letters.

A, B, C, D, E, F, G, H, I, J, K, L, M, N, O, P, Q, R, S, T, U, V, W, X, Y, Z

Exercise 3. Listen and circle.

1. Circle the letter *a*.
2. Circle the letter *e*.
3. Circle the letter *i*.
4. Circle the letter *j*.

5. Circle the letter *m*.
6. Circle the letter *p*.
7. Circle the letter *u*.
8. Circle the letter *y*.

Exercise 4. Listen. The consonants are: b, c, d, f, g, h, j, k, l, m, n, p, q, r, s, t, v, w, x, y, and z. The letter *y* has a consonant sound in *you, New York,* and *yes.*

Listen to the vowels: a, e, i, o, u, and y. The letter *y* has a vowel sound in *happy, day,* and *Good-bye.*

Exercise 5. Listen and write the vowels.

1. o, 2. a, 3. i, 4. e, 5. u

Page 4, Names

Exercise 1, Part A. Listen and read.

Man: What's your name?

Woman: Alla.

Man: Could you please repeat that?

Woman: Sure. Alla. A-l-l-a

Page 5, Where Are You From?

Exercise 1, Part A. Listen and read.

Luz: Where are you from?

Yoshi: I'm from Japan. Where are you from?

Luz: I'm from Puerto Rico.

Exercise 2, Part A. Listen and read.

Student A: Who is she?

Student B: That's Alla. She's from Russia.

Student A: Who is he?

Student B: That's Antonio. He's from Colombia.

Page 7, Numbers

Exercise 1. Listen and repeat: 1, 2, 3, 4, 5, 6, 7, 8, 9, 10

Exercise 2. Listen and circle:

a. Circle the number 4. Circle 4.

b. Circle the number 2. Circle 2.

c. Circle the number 5. Circle 5.

d. Circle the number 3. Circle 3.

e. Circle the number 7. Circle 7.

f. Circle the number 6. Circle 6.

g. Circle the number 9. Circle 9.

h. Circle the number 8. Circle 8.

Exercise 3. Listen and write.

a. Write the number 3. Write 3.

b. Write the number 2. Write 2.

c. Write the number 10. Write 10.

d. Write the number 1. Write 1.

e. Write the number 5. Write 5.

f. Write the number 6. Write 6.

g. Write the number 4. Write 4.

h. Write the number 9. Write 9.

i. Write the number 7. Write 7.

j. Write the number 8. Write 8.

Exercise 4. Listen and write the telephone numbers.

a. Write area code (617) 359-1060. Area code (617) 359-1060.

b. Write area code (413) 552-6780. Area code (413) 552-6780.

c. Write area code (212) 733-6104. Area code (212) 733-6104.

d. Write area code (866) 945-1976. Area code (866) 945-1976.

Page 8, Telling Time

Exercise 2, Part A. Listen and write the time.

1. It's five o'clock. *(Repeat.)*

2. It's seven-thirty. *(Repeat.)*

3. It's ten o'clock. *(Repeat.)*

4. It's two-ten. *(Repeat.)*

5. It's eight o'clock. *(Repeat.)*

6. It's nine-thirty. *(Repeat.)*

Page 9, Words for the Classroom

Exercise 1. Listen and repeat the statements.

1. Read.

2. Write your telephone number.

3. Say a number.

4. Repeat the vowels.

5. Look at the blackboard.

6. Point to a number.

7. Ask a question.

8. Answer a question.

9. Take turns.

UNIT 1: AT SCHOOL

CHAPTER 1: NEW FRIENDS

Page 12, Grammar in Action, Reading and Listening

Part A. Here are three conversations. Listen and read.

Conversation 1:

Woman: Hi. I'm Dae Won. I'm from Korea.

Man: My name is Ahmet. I'm from Turkey.

Woman: It's nice to meet you.

Man: It's nice to meet you, too.

Conversation 2:

Student 1: Who is that?

Student 2: Her name is Dae Won.

Student 1: Where is she from?

Student 2: She's from Seoul. It's in Korea.

Conversation 3:

Student 1: Who is that?

Student 2: His name is Ahmet.

Student 1: Where is he from?

Student 2: He's from Ankara. It's in Turkey.

CHAPTER 2: THE CLASSROOM

Page 22, Grammar in Action, Reading and Listening

Listen and read.

Sonia: Hi! I'm Sonia, and this is Jenny. We're in Room 105.

Jenny: This is our classroom. These are our classmates.

Sonia: There is a clock in our classroom. There is a map in our classroom. There is a blackboard in our classroom. There is a computer in our classroom.

Jenny: There are desks in our classroom. There are chairs in our classroom. There are books in our classroom. There are students in our classroom.

Page 25, Exercise 2. Listen for Singular and Plural Nouns

Listen to the sentences. Is the noun plural? Then add –*s*.

1. There is a window in our classroom. *(Repeat.)*
2. There are two pictures. *(Repeat.)*
3. These letters are for you. *(Repeat.)*)
4. This is the blackboard. *(Repeat.)*
5. These are my notebooks. *(Repeat.)*
6. The computers are in the lab. *(Repeat.)*

7. Luis is my classmate. *(Repeat.)*

8. There is a calendar on the wall. *(Repeat.)*

9. There are two calculators. *(Repeat.)*

10. They have new wallets. *(Repeat.)*

11. There's a wastebasket in the room. *(Repeat.)*

12. This is my pencil. *(Repeat.)*

Page 26, Exercise 5. Numbers

Listen and repeat: 11, 12, 13, 14, 15, 16, 17, 18, 19, 20, 21, 22, 23, 24, 25, 26, 27, 28, 29, 30

Page 27, Talking the Talk

Listen to the pronunciation of these numbers: 13 (/thir-TEEN/) –30 (/THIR-dee/);

14 (/fort-TEEN/) – 40 (/FOR-dee/); 15 (/fif-TEEN/) – 50 (/FIF-tee/);

16 (/six-TEEN/) – 60 (/SIX-tee/); 17 (/seven-TEEN/) – 70 (/SEVEN-dee/);

18 (/eight-TEEN/) – 80 (/EIGH-dee/); 19 (/nine-TEEN/) – 90 (/NINE-dee/)

Page 27, Exercise 6. Listening for Numbers and Nouns

Part A. Listen and circle the number in the sentence.

1. There are thirteen people. *(Repeat.)*

2. There are 30 students in the class. *(Repeat.)*

3. Look at page 40. *(Repeat.)*

4. He is 15 years old. *((Repeat.)*

5. There are 16 classrooms. *(Repeat.)*

6. She is 70 years old. *(Repeat.)*

7. I have $18.00. *(Repeat.)*

8. There are 90 pages in the book. *(Repeat.)*

Part B. Listen and write the number (from 1 to 30). Circle the noun.

1. There are 12 students here. *(Repeat.)*

2. There are 25 notebooks on the desk. *(Repeat.)*

3. There are two maps in the book. *(Repeat.)*

4. There are twenty pieces of chalk here. *(Repeat.)*

5. The teacher has three erasers. *(Repeat.)*

6. One man in the class is from China. *(Repeat.)*

7. Thirteen women are from Mexico. *(Repeat.)*

8. There is one TV in the room. *(Repeat.)*.

9. He has 30 CDs. *(Repeat.)*

10. There are 11 backpacks on the floor. *(Repeat.)*

11. There are 14 pens on the desk. *(Repeat.)*

12. I have 19 classmates. *(Repeat.)*

13. The students have 16 desks. *(Repeat.)*

14. There are 15 names on the list. *(Repeat.)*

Page 32, Exercise 15. Asking and Answering Questions with *What*

Part A. Listen and read.

Student 1: What's this?

Student 2: It's a dictionary.

Student 1: What are these?

Student 2: They're keys.

Student 1: How do you spell that?

Student 2: k-e-y-s

Student 1: Thanks.

UNIT 2: AT HOME

CHAPTER 3: FAMILIES

Page 42, Grammar in Action, Reading and Listening

Part A. Listen and read the conversation.

Irene: Diego, are you married?

Diego: Yes, I am. Here's a picture of my wife.

Irene: What's her name?

Diego: Carmen.

Irene: Do you have children?

Diego: Yes, I have two, one boy and one girl. Here's a picture of them.

Irene: How old are they?

Diego: My son, Manuel, is four years old, and my daughter, Luisa, is two.

Irene: You have a beautiful family.

Diego: Thank you.

Page 43, Think about Grammar

Exercise A. Read the sentences. Then listen and circle the sentence you hear.

1. Are you married? *(Repeat.)*
2. This is my wife. *(Repeat.)*
3. Do you have children? *(Repeat.)*
4. Is this your son? *(Repeat.)*
5. How old is your son? *(Repeat.)*
6. This is my daughter. *(Repeat.)*

Page 43, Exercise B.

Listen to Irene. Circle Diego's answers.

1. Are you married? *(Repeat.)*
2. Do you have children? *(Repeat.)*
3. What's this? *(Repeat.)*
4. How old is your son? *(Repeat.)*
5. Is this your daughter? *(Repeat.)*
6. You have a beautiful family. *(Repeat.)*

Page 52, Exercise 12. *Do You Have* **Questions and Answers**

Listen to the questions. Say your answer: *Yes, I do.* **or** *No, I don't.*

1. Do you have a desk? *(Repeat.)*
2. Do you have a book? *(Repeat.)*
3. Do you have a notebook? *(Repeat.)*
4. Do you have a backpack? *(Repeat.)*
5. Do you have a watch? *(Repeat.)*

6. Do you have a cell phone? *(Repeat.)*
7. Do you have a TV? *(Repeat.)*
8. Do you have a car? *(Repeat.)*
9. Do you have $10.00? *(Repeat.)*

CHAPTER 4: NICE EYES AND A GREAT SMILE

Page 55, Grammar in Action, Reading and Listening

Part A. Listen and read the conversation.

Noriko: That's a good picture, Irene.

Diego: Is that your boyfriend?

Irene: No! It's my brother David.

Noriko: He's handsome.

Irene: I don't think so!

Noriko: Oh, yes, he is! He has nice eyes and a great smile.

Diego: Is he older or younger than you?

Irene: Younger. I'm 19, and he's 17. We have an older brother, too. He's 22.

Diego: What is that brother's name?

Irene: John. That's my father's name, too.

Page 56, Think about Grammar

Part B. Listen to the questions about Irene and David. Circle your answers.

1. Who is in the picture, Irene's boyfriend or her brother? *(Repeat.)*
2. Who is older, Irene or David? *(Repeat.)*
3. Who is younger? *(Repeat.)*
4. How old is David? *(Repeat.)*
5. Do they have an older brother or an older sister? *(Repeat.)*
6. Is David handsome? *(Repeat.)*
7. Does he have a nice smile? *(Repeat.)*

UNIT 3: BUSY PEOPLE

CHAPTER 5: WHAT ARE YOU DOING?

Page 76, Grammar in Action, Reading and Listening

Part A. Listen and read.

Narrator: It's 6:00 on Monday evening. Oscar and Susan are at home. They're in the kitchen, and the radio is playing. Oscar is sitting at the table. He's holding the baby. They're having supper. *(Ring!)* The phone is ringing. Listen to the conversation.

Susan: Hello?

Brian: Hi, Susan!

Susan:	Oh, hi, Brian! How are you?
Brian:	I'm fine, thanks. Listen, what are you doing? Is this a good time to talk, or are you busy? I'm calling about the party for Mom and Dad.
Susan:	Well, we're eating right now.
Brian:	OK, you're busy! So, I'll call back. Say hi to Oscar.
Susan:	OK. I'll talk to you later.
Brian:	Bye!
Susan:	Bye-bye.

Page 89, Talking the Talk

Sometimes the –*es* or –*s* on a plural noun adds a syllable, for example: one house, two houses. *House* has one syllable; *houses* has two syllables. Listen: one hairbrush, two hairbrushes. *Hairbrush* has two syllables; *hairbrushes* has three syllables. Listen again: lunch, lunches; face, faces; message, messages; box, boxes.

Page 90, Exercise 14. Singular vs. Plural Nouns; Pronunciation of Plural Nouns

Part C. Listen and check your answers to Parts A and B. Practice saying the nouns with your partner.

1. couches - yes
2. cats - no
3. socks - no
4. tables - no
5. sandwiches - yes
6. chips - no
7. glasses - yes
8. pieces - yes

CHAPTER 6: WHAT ABOUT YOU?

Page 93, Grammar in Action, Reading and Listening

Part A. Listen and read.

Narrator:	It's Tuesday morning at 9:00. The teacher, Mr. Allen, is beginning his class. Some students aren't in class today. They're absent. Mr. Allen is asking about them.
Mr. Allen:	Where's Miho? Is she absent today?
Miho:	No, I'm here!
Mr. Allen:	Oh, good morning, Miho. Let's see . . . Vitaly isn't here. Is he in school today?
Katya:	No, he isn't. He's not feeling well.
Mr. Allen:	I'm sorry to hear that. What about Idelia? Is she sick, too?
Miho:	She's not sick, but she can't come today. Her children don't have school, and she's staying home with them.
Mr. Allen:	Oh, that's too bad.
Katya:	I can give her the homework.
Mr. Allen:	Can you do that? Good. And what about Oscar? He's absent, too.
Juan:	Oscar can't come today. His car isn't running.
Mr. Allen:	That's too bad! Well, we have a small class today.

Page 97, Talking the Talk

The /a/ in *can* is usually a very short sound. The /a/ in *can't* is a long sound. Write: I can see it. Say: I /kn/ SEE it. Write: I can't see it. Say: I /KANT/ SEE it.

Page 98, Exercise 4. Pronunciation of *Can* vs. *Can't*

Part A. Listen and repeat.

1. I can drive. I can't drive.
2. He can sing. He can't sing.
3. I can cook. I can't cook.
4. We can swim. We can't swim.
5. He can speak English. He can't speak English.
6. The baby can talk. The baby can't talk.

Part B. Listen and circle the letter of the sentence you hear.

1. She can sing. *(Repeat.)*
2. He can't sing. *(Repeat.)*
3. I can't drive. *(Repeat.)*
4. She can drive. *(Repeat.)*
5. They can't do it. *(Repeat.)*
6. We can do it. *(Repeat.)*
7. The baby can talk. *(Repeat.)*
8. He can't dance. *(Repeat.)*

Page 102, Exercise 9. Listen for Conjunctions

Listen to the conversation. Write the word you hear: *and, but,* or *or*.

Miho: Oscar, Katya and I are having a party. Can you and Susan come?

Oscar: Sounds great! When?

Miho: I think on Friday night or maybe on Saturday. We're not sure.

Oscar: Friday's good, but Saturday isn't. We have a babysitter on Friday but not on Saturday.

Miho: That's OK—bring the baby!

Oscar: What else can we bring?

Miho: Oh, something to eat or drink. We'll have pizza and soda and chips or popcorn—things like that.

Oscar: Sounds good. What time?

Miho: I'll call you later!

Oscar: OK.

UNIT 4: EVERYDAY LIFE

CHAPTER 7: DAILY ROUTINES

Page 112, Grammar in Action, Reading and Listening

Part A. Listen and read.

Narrator: It's 8:30 on Tuesday morning. Angie is waiting for the bus. She's going to school.

Angie: Hi, Martin! What are you doing on the bus? You always drive to school.

Martin: Yes, but today, my brother's using my car. He sometimes borrows it.

Angie: I see.

Martin: Do you take the bus every day?

Angie: No, not every day, just on Tuesdays and Thursdays.

Martin: What about the other days? Do you have a car?

Angie: Yes, we do, but my husband needs it for his job. I usually get a ride from a friend, sometimes from Zulma.

Martin: She drives an old blue Chevy, right?

Angie: Yeah, it's REALLY old, but it runs!

Page 118, Talking the Talk

Sometimes the -*es* or -*s* at the end of a verb adds a syllable, for example: use, uses. *Use* has one syllable. *Uses* has two syllables. Listen to these examples: kiss, kisses; fix, fixes. I watch TV. He watches TV.

Page 118, Exercise 6. Pronunciation of Verbs

Part B. Listen to the statements. Check your answers to Part A.

1. I live on Green Street. She lives on Green St. (no)
2. They teach English. He teaches English. (yes)
3. We miss our friends. He misses his friends. (yes)
4. You listen in class. She listens in class. (no)
5. We eat fruit. It eats fruit. (no)
6. They fix cars. He fixes cars. (yes)
7. You study math. She studies math. (no)
8. They finish at 10:00. It finishes at 10:00. (yes)
9. I play basketball. He plays basketball. (no)
10. We use computers. She uses computers. (yes)

Page 122, Exercise 11. *Yes/No* Questions and Short Answers

Part B. Listen to the conversation. Check your answers to Part A.

Mrs. Smith: Do you and your sister work at McDonalds?

Julie: Yes, we do. We both work there part-time.

Mrs. Smith: What do you do, Julie? Do you make hamburgers?

Julie: No, I don't. I work at the cash register.

Mrs. Smith: I see. So, do you take orders for food?

Julie: Yes, I do. I take the orders, and people pay me.

Mrs. Smith: What about your sister? Does she work at the register, too?

Julie: Yes, she does. Kate sometimes works in the kitchen, too.

Mrs. Smith: Do you like working at McDonalds?

Julie: Yes, I do. I see lots of my friends there, and I like the food.

Mrs. Smith: What about Kate? Does she like working there?

Julie: No, she doesn't. She's getting tired of hamburgers and french fries!

Page 122, Talking the Talk

There are many ways to answer "Yes" or "No." For example, ask the question "Do you work full-time?" In formal conversation, people often answer "Yes, I do" or "No, I don't." In informal conversation, people often answer "Yes" by saying "Uh-huh," "Yup," or "Yeah," and they often answer "No" by saying "Uh-uh," "Nope," or "Nah."

Page 123, Exercise 12. Informal Ways to Answer *Yes* and *No*

Listen to the informal conversations. You will hear each conversation twice (two times). Does the speaker answer *Yes* or *No*? Circle your answers.

Conversation 1:

Woman: Does Jack work at the bank?

Man: Uh-huh.

Again: *(Repeat.)*

Conversation 2:

Man: Do you know Dr. Rose?

Man: Nope.

Again: *(Repeat.)*

Conversation 3:

Woman: Do you like my hair like this?

Woman: Yeah!

Again: *(Repeat.)*

Conversation 4:

Man: Does she speak Japanese?

Woman: Uh-uh.

Again: *(Repeat.)*

Conversation 5:

Woman: Do you go shopping with your girlfriend?

Man: Nah.

Again: *(Repeat.)*

Conversation 6:

Man: Does he like his job?

Woman: Yup.

Again: *(Repeat.)*

CHAPTER 8: WOULD YOU LIKE SOMETHING?

Page 129, Grammar in Action, Reading and Listening

Part A. Listen and read.

Narrator: Angie, Martin, and Zulma are at school. It's almost time for class, but they have ten minutes. They're in the cafeteria.

Angie: I need more coffee! Martin, would you like some more?

Martin: No, thanks. I'm fine.

Angie: Zulma, what about you? Would you like something to drink?

Zulma: What do they have? I don't usually drink coffee.

Angie: They have orange juice, there's tea, . . .

Zulma: Oh, I'd like some tea. Thanks.

Angie: No problem.

Martin: My wife never drinks coffee. It always gives her headaches.

Zulma: It doesn't give me headaches, but I don't like the taste!

Page 132, Exercise 2, Making Negative Statements

Part A. Read the statements about Angie and Phil. Listen to the story. Are the statements true or false? Check your answers.

Angie and Phil live in a small apartment. It has one bedroom, and the kitchen is small. Phil doesn't like the kitchen, and he doesn't like to cook. Angie likes to cook, and she makes dinner every night. Angie and Phil both enjoy good food. After dinner, Phil washes the dishes. They always eat at home. They don't go to restaurants.

UNIT 5: GOING PLACES

CHAPTER 9: IT'S SUNNY AND WARM

Page 150, Grammar in Action, Reading and Listening

Part A. Listen and read.

Narrator: Yuki and Kazumi are at the airport. They see their friend Manuel. He's waiting in line. They're surprised to see him, and he's surprised to see them.

Yuki: Look who's in front of us!

Kazumi: Manuel! Hello! Where are you going?

Manuel: Hi! I'm going to Puerto Rico, to see my mother. I always visit her in December.

Yuki: Yeah, when it gets cold and snowy around here . . .

Manuel: . . . and it's sunny and warm down there!

Kazumi: Where does your mother live?

Manuel: In Bayamón. It's near San Juan. And what about you? What are you doing at the airport?

Yuki: We're going to Mexico.

Kazumi: For a week at the beach!

Manuel: That sounds great. Have fun!

Kazumi: Thanks—you, too.

Page 154, Exercise 4. Talking about the Time and the Weather

Part A. Look at the pictures. Listen to the conversation. Who is talking? Choose picture 1, 2, or 3.

Man: Hello?

Woman: Hello! Tom, is that you?

Man: Sue? Hi—I can hardly hear you.

Woman: Yes, it's me!

Man: Are you at home?

Woman: No, I'm on my way to the airport. It's 8:00 here.

Man: How's the weather there?

Woman: Not good! It's very dark and cloudy.

Man: I can't hear you—I'm on the street, and it's windy here. Are you in the car?

Woman: Yes. I'll call you back.

Man: OK!

Page 159, Exercise 9. Prepositions for Describing Location or Place

Part A. Look at the picture. The Johnsons are on vacation. They're staying at a hotel near the beach. Listen to the statements, and circle True or False.

1. The Johnsons are staying at a hotel. *(Repeat.)*
2. Their hotel is on Water Street. *(Repeat.)*
3. Their room is on the third floor. *(Repeat.)*
4. There's a park across from their hotel. *(Repeat.)*
5. There's a café in front of the hotel. *(Repeat.)*
6. The café is between a grocery store and a bookstore. *(Repeat.)*
7. A restaurant is across from the bookstore. *(Repeat.)*
8. Green Street is between Market and Center Streets. *(Repeat.)*
9. There are two hotels on Green Street. *(Repeat.)*
10. The Johnsons are staying near the beach. *(Repeat.)*

CHAPTER 10: EATING OUT

Page 165, Grammar in Action, Reading and Listening

Part A. Listen and read.

Narrator: Yuki and Kazumi are at the beach in Mexico.

Kazumi: Are you hungry? Remember, we have a bag of food.

Yuki: I'm starving! What's in the bag?

Kazumi: Well, there's bread and fruit . . .

Yuki: Are there any grapes?

Kazumi: No, we don't have any grapes, but there's watermelon and we have two oranges.

Yuki: The watermelon sounds good. Is there any meat or cheese? To make sandwiches?

Kazumi: We have meat *AND* cheese . . .

Yuki: What kind?

Kazumi: The meat is chicken, and the cheese is . . . I don't know! And we have lettuce and tomatoes, too.

Yuki: Terrific! How many sandwiches can we make?

Kazumi: How much food do you need?!

Yuki: A lot! I always get hungry at the beach.

Page 169, Exercise 3. Subject Nouns and Singular/Plural Verbs

Part B. Listen to the conversation in Part A. Check your answers.

Nancy is telling her friends to come into the kitchen.

Nancy: Hey, everybody! Come and eat—the food is on the table!

Bill: Wow, all this food looks great.

Nancy: The drinks are in the refrigerator. The milk is on the top shelf. The orange juice is next to the milk, and there is soda on the bottom shelf. The soda cans are cold, I think, but there is ice in the freezer if you want it. The iced tea has lemon but no sugar in it—the sugar is on the table. I can make coffee, too.

Dan: Ahh, coffee! That sounds good. Thanks.

Page 176, Exercise 10. Questions with *How Much/How Many*; Quantifiers

Part A. Listen to the conversation. Check the things the nurse asks about.

Nurse: Well, Mr. Feldman, I'd like to ask you a few questions.

Mr. Feldman: Sure!

Nurse: OK, how much coffee do you drink in a day?

Mr. Feldman: Oh, I don't know. About eight cups, I guess.

Nurse: Eight cups? Hmmm, that's a lot of coffee. How much water do you drink?

Mr. Feldman: Water?! Very little. I almost never drink it.

Nurse: I see. OK, how many eggs do you eat in a week?

Mr. Feldman: Oh, I love eggs. Have two or three of 'em for breakfast every day.

Nurse: Two or three a day . . . that means you eat 15 to 20 eggs a week?

Mr. Feldman: That's right.

Nurse: OK. Now, how many servings of vegetables?

Mr. Feldman: Well, not many. I like potatoes, but I don't really eat many vegetables.

Nurse: How much fruit do you eat?

Mr. Feldman: Oh, maybe one piece. An apple, or maybe an orange.

Nurse: Do you mean one piece of fruit a day?

Mr. Feldman: No, one a week.

Nurse: I see. Do you smoke, Mr. Feldman?

Mr. Feldman: Yup, I'm a smoker.

Nurse: How many cigarettes do you smoke in a day?

Mr. Feldman: A pack a day.

Nurse: So, that's 20 cigarettes a day, eight cups of coffee, lots of eggs . . . Mr. Feldman, I'm worried about you. We need to have a talk.

Part B. Listen again. Write quantifiers in the chart for Mr. Feldman's answers. *(The conversation repeats.)*

UNIT 6: LOOKING BACK

CHAPTER 11: WHAT A WEEKEND!

Page 186, Grammar in Action, Reading and Listening

Part A. Listen and read.

Henry: Hi, Debbie! How was your weekend?

Debbie: Oh, the usual. I cleaned the house, shopped, and cooked. Yesterday we played some tennis. That's all. What about you? How was your weekend?

Henry: My weekend was like a bad dream.

Debbie: What?! What do you mean?

Henry: Well, Eva went to her parents' house for the weekend, because they were sick . . .

Debbie: So you were home alone with the kids?

Henry: Yup. And Friday evening, the baby got an ear infection, so I took her to the hospital.

Debbie: Poor thing!

Henry: We were there for HOURS. She cried all night, but she was fine the next day. Then Max was in a fight and got a black eye . . .

Debbie: Oh, dear!

Henry: And yesterday, Joey had an accident with the car.

Debbie: I hope he's OK!

Henry: He's fine. He wasn't hurt—nobody was hurt—and it wasn't his fault. But I was pretty upset . . .

Debbie: I can imagine! Boy, what a weekend!

Page 192, Exercise 5. Questions and Answers with *Was/Were*

Part B. Listen to the conversation between two students, Steve and Josh. Circle the answers.

Steve: Hey, Josh!

Josh: Hey, Steve. How ya doin?

Steve: Not bad. Listen, were you at the basketball game Saturday night?

Josh: No, were you? I was at a concert.

Steve: Yeah? What concert? Where was it?

Josh: At Ward Stadium. It was the Stompers concert.

Steve: The Stompers?! Cool. How was it?

Josh: It was great! But there weren't many people there.

Steve: Really? I'm surprised. The Stompers are huge. How much were tickets?

Josh: $100 and up.

Steve: You're kidding! Well, that explains it. That's a lotta money. I'm surprised YOU were there.

Page 196, Talking the Talk

1. Sometimes the *-ed* ending adds a syllable. This happens when the base verb ends in the sound /t/ or /d/. Listen to these examples: hate, hated; need, needed; expect, expected.

2. Sometimes the *-ed* ending on a verb doesn't sound like /d/. It sounds like /t/.

   Listen to these examples: talked, watched, kissed, washed, laughed, stopped, fixed.

   See Appendix 7 for more information.

Page 196, Exercise 11. Pronunciation of –ed Verb Endings

Part A. Listen to the sentences. Does the verb ending sound like /d/ or /t/?

1. Joe partied on Friday night. *(Repeat.)*
2. He stayed in bed late. *(Repeat.)*
3. He cleaned up the apartment. *(Repeat.)*
4. He shopped at Dino's Market. *(Repeat.)*
5. He washed a lot of clothes. *(Repeat.)*
6. He played a video game. *(Repeat.)*
7. He watched a game on TV. *(Repeat.)*
8. He worked out. *(Repeat.)*
9. He studied at the library. *(Repeat.)*
10. He called his parents. *(Repeat.)*

Part C. Listen to the verbs from Part B. Check your answers.

1. I learned about the concert from an ad on the radio. - No
2. I waited in line for the show. - Yes
3. I needed to buy a ticket. - Yes
4. I wanted to see the singer. - Yes
5. I expected to enjoy the concert. - Yes
6. I enjoyed it very much. - No

CHAPTER 12: LONG AGO

Page 201, Grammar in Action, Reading and Listening

Part A. Listen and read.

Henry: So, Daniel, you're from Taiwan, aren't you?

Daniel: Yes, that's right. I was born in Taipei.

Henry: Where did you grow up?

Daniel: In Taipei. My parents still live there.

Henry: And when did you come to the U.S.?

Daniel: I came about a year ago. I wanted to work in international business, but I didn't speak much English.

Henry: Did you start to learn English just last year?!

Daniel: Oh, no! I started in third grade. But for a long time, I didn't take it seriously. At the university, I began to think about my future. Then I met my wife and decided to come here to study.

Henry: Did she come with you?

Daniel: Oh, of course! And our baby, too.

Page 204, Talking the Talk

People sometimes pronounce *did you* as "didja" or "ja." For example, write "Did you have fun?" But you will often hear "'Didja' have fun?" or "'Ja' have fun?"

Page 208, Exercise 6. Simple Past Tense Statements, Irregular Verbs

Part B. Listen to the whole story of Snow White.

This is the story of Snow White. Once upon a time, long ago, Snow White lived with her mean and cruel stepmother. Her stepmother hated her because Snow White was beautiful. The poor girl was very unhappy, so she left home, and she ran into the forest. She ran and ran through the forest. Then she came to a little house. She went into the house. It was very messy, so she began cleaning. After a while, she decided to take a rest. There were seven little beds upstairs. Snow White went to sleep there. Then the owners of the little house came home. They were seven little men: the Seven Dwarves. They saw Snow White on the bed. She opened her eyes and saw them, too. They were all very surprised. The dwarves were nice to Snow White, and she stayed at their house and was happy there. Then, one day, her stepmother came to the house. Snow White didn't know it was her stepmother. She looked like a nice old woman. She had an apple for Snow White, but it was a poisoned apple. The girl ate it, and she went to sleep. She slept and slept, and the dwarves were very sad. Many years went by. Then one day, a handsome prince came into the forest. He saw Snow White, and he kissed her. She opened her eyes. Then Snow White and the prince lived happily ever after.

UNIT 7: LET'S LOOK AHEAD

CHAPTER 13: LOOKING AHEAD TO THE FUTURE

Page 220, Grammar in Action, Reading and Listening

Part A. Listen and read.

Mrs. Scott: My daughter's going to come home from college next week.

Nestor: Great! I bet you're looking forward to seeing her. What's she studying these days?

Mrs. Scott: She's taking a lot of science courses—chemistry, physics. . . .

Nestor: Is she going to be a scientist? or a doctor?

Mrs. Scott: No, she's not. My son Johnny is going to be a doctor, but Janelle has other ideas.

Nestor: What is she going to do?

Mrs. Scott: In a few years, she's going to be an astronaut.

Nestor: Really?! Wow. . . . Why is she going to do that?

Mrs. Scott: Well, Janelle says, in the future, space is going to be very important. More and more people are probably going to travel there. And she wants to be one of them!

Nestor: Is she going to walk on the moon?

Mrs. Scott: It's possible . . . who knows?! Maybe we're all going to go there.

Nestor: No way! Not me!

Page 223, Talking the Talk

The *going to* in sentences with *be going to* often sounds like "gonna." For example, write "They are going to win." But you will often hear "They're 'gonna' win."

CHAPTER 14: PLANS AND PREDICTIONS

Page 232, Grammar in Action, Reading and Listening

Part A. Listen and read.

Narrator: Johnny Scott is talking to his sister Janelle on the phone. He's at home, and she's at college. Johnny has a problem, and he wants her help.

Johnny: Janelle, listen, I have to talk to you. I decided something last night. I'm going to go to music school next year.

Janelle: Good for you! I know you never really wanted to be a doctor.

Johnny: But what'll I do? I can't tell Mom and Dad. They'll kill me!

Janelle: No, they won't. They'll understand.

Johnny: Will you tell them?

Janelle: No, Johnny, you have to do it. But, don't worry, it'll be fine.

Johnny: Janelle!

Janelle: OK, maybe they won't like it at first. Dad will probably need a little time . . . OK, Johnny, wait and tell them when I get home. We'll do it together.

Johnny: When will you be here?

Janelle: Next week.

Page 235, Exercise 2. Affirmative and Negative Statements with *Will*

Part A. Listen to the forecast (predictions about the weather). Draw pictures or write words for the weather each day (for example, *sunny, cloudy, rainy*).

Good morning, everyone! This is Dave Powers with your Monday morning Channel 7 Weather Report. Let's take a look at today's forecast AND our forecast for the coming week. Today, we won't see much of that sun—it's going to be cool and cloudy all through the day. Tomorrow will be a little nicer. In fact, it'll be warm and sunny all day on Tuesday. On Wednesday, the warm weather will continue. We'll see another sunny day. Looking ahead to Thursday: there'll be some clouds in the morning, and we'll see some rain that afternoon. Yes, folks, a cloudy morning on Thursday, followed by some rain, possibly heavy at times. Then on Friday, the sun will be back. That's right: Friday will give us a nice start to a sunny weekend!

Page 241, Talking the Talk

In conversation, *have to* often sounds like "hafta." *Has to* often sounds like "hasta." For example, write "I have to go now." You will often hear "I 'hafta' go now." Write "She has to work at 9:00." You will often hear "She 'hasta' work at 9:00."

Page 242, Exercise 9. Affirmative Statements with *Have to*

Part A. Janelle is a college student. It's time for her to register for classes for next semester. Listen to the information about registering for classes. Listen again and check the things Janelle has to do.

Janelle is a college student. It's time for her to register for classes for next semester. Which classes is she going to take? She has to choose her courses. How does she choose? First, she has to get information about courses. Janelle has to talk to other students. This is important. She can ask other students, *Who's a good teacher?* and *Is this a good course?* Janelle can also read the course catalogue. The course catalogue is a book that tells about all the classes at the college. Janelle can look at the catalogue *OR* she can use her computer. She can read the information online. It's her choice. Then, Janelle has to make an appointment with her advisor. That's easy. She doesn't need to call. She can go to her advisor's office and put her name on the sign-up sheet. It's probably on the door to the office. Janelle has to talk about her courses with her advisor. She also has to fill out a course registration form. She has to write her name, her student ID number, the course numbers, and so on. Her advisor has to sign the form. Finally, Janelle has to take the form to the Registrar's Office.

Index

A/an, 57, 168
Adjectives
    descriptive, 61
    possessive, 16, 28
Adverbs of frequency, 136
A few, 174
Affirmative statements
    with *be going to*, 222
    with *be*, present tense, 15, 28
    with *be*, simple past tense, 188
    with *can*, 97
    with *have*, 49
    with *have to*, 240
    with *will*, 234
    present progressive verbs in, 78
    simple past tense in, 194, 207
    simple present tense in, 114
A little, 174
A lot of, 174
Alphabet, 2
Always, 136
And, 101
Answers to *yes/no* questions, 122
Any, 174
Articles
    a/an, 57, 167
    indefinite, 167
    the, 170
Asking for something politely, 138
At for location, 158
At night, 155

Base form of the verb, 81
Be
    past tense of, 188, 191
    present tense of, 15, 28, 44, 46
    there + be, 30, 172, 188
Be going to, 222
    affirmative statements, 222
    negative statements, 222
    vs. *will*, 238
    wh- questions and answers, 227
    yes/no questions and short answers, 225
But, 101

Can
    affirmative and negative statements, 97
    pronunciation of *can/can't*, 97
    yes/no questions and short answers, 99
Cannot, 97
Capital letters, 2, 3
Commas, before conjunctions, 101
Conjunctions *and*, *but*, and *or*, 101
Consonants, 2, 57, 81, 194
Contractions
    in the present progressive, 78, 83, 95
    in the simple past tense, 203, 205
    in the simple present tense, 121, 131
    with *be*, 15, 18, 30, 44, 46
    with *be going to*, 222
    with *will*, 234
    with *would*, 138
Count nouns, 88, 167
Cursive letters, 3

Date, telling the, 152
Day, telling the, 152
Definite article *the*, 170
Descriptive adjectives, 61
Did you . . . in spoken English, 203
Do/does
    in simple present tense affirmative statements, 116
    in *wh-* questions, 133
    in *yes/no* questions and short answers, 121
Don't/doesn't, 131

-(e)d ending on simple past verbs
    spelling rules for, 194
    in spoken English, 196
-(e)s ending on plural nouns, 88, 89, A-3
-(e)s ending on third person singular verbs, 116
Expressing necessity with *have to*, 240

Expressing the future, 222, 234

Few, a, 174
Functions
    of *be going to*, 238
    of the present progressive, 78, 124
    of the simple present, 124
    of *will*, 234, 236
Future time expressions, 224
Future time. *See Be going to, Will.*

Go, 116. *See also Be going to.*

Has, 49. *See also Have, Have to.*
Have. See also Have to.
    affirmative statements with, simple present, 49, 116
    in questions with *Do you have*, 51
Have to
    in affirmative statements, 240
    in spoken English, 240
How many, 51, 174
How much, 174
How often, 133
How old, 46
How was/were, 191

I'd like, 138
In
    + a month, 155
    + an amount of time, 224
    + a part of the day, 155
    for location, 158
Indefinite article *a/an*, 57, 168
-ing. See Present progressive.
Irregular plural nouns, 24, 88
Irregular verbs
    simple past tense, 197, 203, 205, 207, 209
    simple present tense, 116
Is/Are there. See There + be.
It + the time, day, date, or weather, 152
Its vs. *it's*, 153

Know, 124

Letters of the alphabet, 2, 3
Like, 124
Little, a, 174
Location or place, prepositions
    for, 158
Lot of, a, 174

Making an offer, 138
Many, 174
Much, 174

Need, 124
Negative statements
    present progressive, 95
    present tense of *be*, 44
    simple past tense, 205
    simple past tense of *be*, 188
    simple present tense, 131
    with *be going to*, 222
    with *can*, 97
    with *will*, 234
Never, 136
Next + a period of time, 224
Non-action verbs, 124
Noncount nouns, 88, 167, 168
Nouns
    common and proper, 24
    count, 88, 167
    -(e)s ending in spoken English,
        89
    noncount, 88, 167, 168
    possessive, 64
    spelling rules for *-(e)s* ending,
        89
    singular and plural, 24
    with irregular plurals, 24, 88
    with plural form only, 88
No, ways to say, 122
Numbers, 7, 26, 27, A-1

Object pronouns, 161
Objects of prepositions, 155
Offers, 138, 139, 238
Often, 136
On
    + a day, 155
    for place or location, 158
Or, 101

Past time expressions, 189
Place or location, prepositions for,
    158

Plural nouns, 24, 88
Polite offers and requests, 139
Possessive adjectives, 16, 28
Possessive nouns, 64
Predictions, 238
Prepositional phrases, 155
Prepositions, 155
    for describing location or
        place, 158
    for describing time, 155
    objects of, 155
Present continuous. *See* Present
    progressive.
Present progressive
    affirmative statements, 78
    negative statements, 95
    questions with *what*, 83
    use of, 78
    vs. simple present, 124
    yes/no questions and short
        answers, 83
Present tense verbs. *See* Simple
    present tense, present
    progressive.
Pronouns
    object, 161
    subject, 14, 28, 161
Pronunciation
    of *can/can't*, 97
    of *did you*, 203
    of *-(e)d* ending on simple past
        verbs, 196
    of *-(e)s* ending on nouns, 89
    of *-(e)s* ending on verbs, 115
    of *going to* in *be going to*, 222
    of numbers, 27
    of *there, their,* and *they're*, 173
    of *What/Where* + *does*, 134

Quantifiers, 174
Questions. *See Be, Be going to, Can,
    Have,* Present progressive,
    Simple past tense, Simple
    present tense, *Will*.

Regular verbs, simple past tense,
    194, 203, 205, 209
Requests, 138, 139
Responding to an offer, 138

-s ending on plural nouns, 88, A-3
-s ending on third-person singular
    verbs, simple present tense,
    114, 116

Short answers. *See Be, Be going to,
    Can, Have,* Present
    progressive, Simple past
    tense, Simple present tense,
    Will.
Short forms. *See* Contractions.
Simple past tense
    affirmative statements, 194
    of *be*, 188, 191
    -(e)d endings in spoken
        English, 196
    negative statements, 205
    of irregular verbs, 197, 207
    regular verbs, spelling, 194
    wh- questions and answers,
        209
    yes/no questions and short
        answers, 203
Simple present tense
    affirmative statements, 114,
        116
    of *have*, 49
    irregular verbs, 116
    negative statements, 131
    spelling rules for third person
        singular verbs, 116
    uses of, 124
    vs. present progressive, 124
    wh- questions and answers,
        133
    with third person singular
        subjects, 116
    yes/no questions and answers,
        121
Singular, 24
Some, 174
Sometimes, 136
Spelling
    -ing verb forms, 81, A-5
    plural nouns, 88, A-3
    simple past tense of regular
        verbs, 194
    simple present tense verbs, 116
Statements. *See* Affirmative
    statements, Negative
    statements.
Stative verbs. *See* Non-action
    verbs.
Subject pronouns, 14, 28, 161
Subject–verb agreement, 167

That, 59
The, 170
Their, 28, 173

There + be
  past tense statements with, 188
  present tense affirmative
    statements with, 30
  present tense *yes/no* questions
    and short answers with, 172
There. See also There + be.
  in spoken English, 173
These, 31, 59
They're, 28, 173
Third person singular subjects and
    verbs, 114, 116
This, 31, 59
Those, 59
Time expressions
  future, 224
  past, 189
  with present progressive verbs,
    124
  with simple present tense
    verbs, 124
Time, telling, 8, 152

Uses of
  be going to, 238

  the present progressive, 78,
    124
  the simple present, 124
  will, 234, 236
Usually, 126

Vowels, 2, 57, 81, 194

Want, 124
Was, 188, 191
Ways to answer *Yes* or *No,* 122
Weather, describing, 152
Were, 188, 191
Wh- questions and answers
  with *be,* 18, 46, 191
  with *be going to,* 227
  with contractions, 18
  with *How many/how much,* 51,
    174
  with *How was/were,* 191
  simple past tense, 209
  simple present tense, 133
  with *will,* 236
What, 18, 83, 133
What do you do?, 134

What or *Where + does* in spoken
    English, 134
What's in conversation, 83
Where, 18, 133
Who, 18
Whom, 209
Why, 133
Will
  affirmative statements, 234
  contracted forms, 234
  negative statements, 234
  vs. *be going to,* 238
  wh- questions and answers,
    236
  yes/no questions and short
    answers, 236
Would you like, 138

Yes, ways to say, 122
Yes/No questions and answers. *See
    Be, Be going to, Can, Have,
    present progressive, simple
    past tense, simple present
    tense, There + be, Will.*